ENGLISH PLACE-NAME SOCIETY. VOLUME I. PART II

THE CHIEF ELEMENTS USED IN ENGLISH PLACE-NAMES

BEING THE SECOND PART OF THE INTRODUCTION TO THE SURVEY *of* ENGLISH PLACE-NAMES

Edited by

ALLEN MAWER

CAMBRIDGE

AT THE UNIVERSITY PRESS

1924

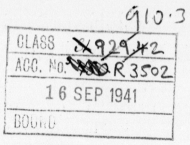
PRINTED IN GREAT BRITAIN

PREFACE

THE main purpose of this volume is to provide a useful companion to the successive county volumes of the English Place-name Survey, by presenting in concise and summary form a good deal of the matter which, as it is in the nature of 'common form,' would otherwise have to be repeated in each successive volume.

The list of elements handled lays no claim to being exhaustive but an attempt has been made to deal with all those elements, English and Scandinavian, which are of anything like common occurrence. No attempt has been made to deal with the Celtic or the French elements, chiefly because they are of comparatively rare occurrence and can be satisfactorily dealt with as they occur in the different counties.

In the interpretation of the English elements the utmost possible use has been made of the material to be found in the Anglo-Saxon charters as printed by Kemble and Birch. In handling that material the work of Professor Toller in his revision and completion of Bosworth's *Anglo-Saxon Dictionary* has been invaluable. The present volume could indeed never have been written were it not for the existence of that dictionary, of the *Oxford English Dictionary*, and Wright's *English Dialect Dictionary*. Other books and articles to which the author must express himself as specially indebted are: Ekwall, *Place-names of Lancashire*, especially pp. 7–21 on 'Elements found in Lancashire Place-names'; Grundy, 'On the meanings of certain terms in the Anglo-Saxon Charters' (*Essays and Studies by members of the English Association*, 8. 36–69); Lindkvist, *Middle English Place-names of Scandinavian origin*; Middendorff, *Altenglisches Flurnamenbuch*; Liebermann, *Die Gesetze der Angelsächsen*.

In addition to the interpretation of the chief elements, an attempt has been made to deal with their distribution, at least in those cases in which a study of their distribution may ultimately throw light on problems of racial settlement and the like.

In the matter of interpretation, and still more in that of distribution, the volume suffers from a heavy but unavoidable handicap. It has had to be written at the beginning of the Survey instead of at the end, as would have been more fitting. Many of the problems with which it deals can never be handled with any hope of success until we have the full evidence at our command, but on the other hand none of the ensuing volumes could have been written without some such preliminary statements as those given here, setting forth the present condition of our knowledge. Many of these statements are clearly in the nature of suggestions rather than assertions and the whole attitude of the author towards them is tentative and exploratory rather than dogmatic or final.

For the study of the distribution of the various elements and illustration of their use, the sources of information have been threefold:

(1) The various books on place-name study already published.

(2) The author's own collections, made for the most part before the Survey was undertaken.

(3) Material placed at his disposal by various helpers and friends of the Survey. Among these he would wish especially to thank the Rev. A. Goodall for his very generous gift to the Survey of his East Riding of Yorkshire collections and interpretations, the late Mr Philip Sturge of Winscombe for extensive gazetteers of Devon and Somerset names with early forms attached, Mr J. E. B. Gover for access to his collection of Cornish material and similar facilities afforded by Mr Schram for Norfolk and Mr P. H. Reaney for Essex.

The use of each element has been illustrated by examples. The purpose of those examples is (1) to illustrate, as far as may be, the various forms under which that suffix may appear disguised in present-day place nomenclature, (2) to arouse interest in the etymology and history of particular names and types of names. No name has been included except on the authority of good early forms, but considerations of space forbade the actual quotation of such.

In using the illustrations given under each element it should be noted that:

(1) Where a p.n. is composed of two elements an attempt has been made to include both its elements. Where a name is entered only under one element it may be inferred either (i) that the first element is a personal name and therefore does not fall within the

scope of this volume, or (ii) that it is of obscure and uncertain origin, or (iii) that it is what it appears to be in the present-day form[1].

(2) No conclusion should be drawn that because a p.n. in any given example has a particular meaning that it therefore has the same meaning elsewhere (cf. Worton s.v. **ofer** and **wyrt**). Even where *passim* is given after a name it only means that that name is found in the sense given in several counties, not that it invariably has that meaning (cf. Broughton s.v. **broc** and **beorg**).

(3) None of the illustrations are exhaustive. An illustration of a name may be given from one county and other examples of the name, of the same form and history, may possibly be found in that county or in other unmentioned counties. It is in the very nature of things that, quite apart from considerations of space, no exhaustive references for the occurrence of any particular name can be given in the present state of our knowledge.

The author's special thanks are due to Professors Ekwall and Tait and to his co-editor for their kindness in reading Part II in proof. It owes much to their watchful care.

A. M.

March, 1924.

---

[1] This necessarily involves a certain measure of ambiguity but to do otherwise would involve the printing of an impossibly large number of illustrations. It should be noted further that cases of (*h*)*all* for *hale* and *borough* for *beorg* in modern p.n. forms have had to be left unnoticed for the same reason.

BIBLIOGRAPHY OF THE CHIEF BOOKS DEALING WITH THE HISTORY OF ENGLISH PLACE-NAMES

ALEXANDER, H. *Place-names of Oxfordshire*, Oxford, 1912.
BADDELEY, W. ST C. *Place-names of Gloucestershire*, Gloucester, 1913.
—— *Place-names of Herefordshire*, Bristol, 1913[1].
BANNISTER, A. T. *Place-names of Herefordshire*, Cambridge, 1913.
BOWCOCK, *Place-names of Shropshire*, Shrewsbury, 1923.
DUIGNAN, W. H. *Notes on Staffordshire Place-names*, Oxford, 1912.
—— *Warwickshire Place-names*, Oxford, 1912.
—— *Worcestershire Place-names*, Oxford, 1905.
EKBLOM, E. *Place-names of Wiltshire*, Uppsala, 1917.
EKWALL, E. *Contributions to the History of OE dialects*, Lund, 1917.
—— *Scandinavians and Celts in the North-West of England*, Lund, 1918.
—— *Place-names of Lancashire*, Manchester, 1922.
—— *English Place-names in -ing*, Lund, 1923.
GOODALL, A. *Place-names of South-West Yorkshire*, Cambridge, 1914.
GOVER, J. E. B. *The Place-names of Middlesex*, London, 1922.
JOHNSTON, J. B. *The Place-names of England and Wales*, London, 1914.
LINDKVIST, H. *Middle English Place-names of Scandinavian Origin*, Uppsala, 1912.
MAWER, A. *Place-names of Northumberland and Durham*, Cambridge, 1920.
McCLURE, E. *British Place-names in their Historical Setting*, London, 1910.
MIDDENDORFF, H. *Altenglisches Flurnamenbuch*, 1902.
MOORMAN, F. W. *Place-names of the West Riding of Yorkshire*, Leeds, 1910.
MUTSCHMANN, H. *Place-names of Nottinghamshire*, Cambridge, 1913.
ROBERTS, R. G. *Place-names of Sussex*, Cambridge, 1914.
SEDGEFIELD, W. J. *Place-names of Cumberland and Westmorland*, Manchester, 1915.
SKEAT, W. W. *Place-names of Bedfordshire*, Cambridge, 1906.
—— *Place-names of Berkshire*, Oxford, 1911.
—— *Place-names of Cambridgeshire*, Cambridge, 1911.
—— *Place-names of Hertfordshire*, Hertford, 1904.
—— *Place-names of Huntingdonshire*, Cambridge, 1904[1].
—— *Place-names of Suffolk*, Cambridge, 1913.
STENTON, F. M. *Place-names of Berkshire*, Reading, 1911.
WALKER, B. *Place-names of Derbyshire*, Derby, 1914–5[1].
WYLD, H. C. and HIRST, T. O. *Place-names of Lancashire*, London, 1911.
ZACHRISSON, R. E. *Anglo-Norman Influence on English Place-names*, Lund, 1909[2].

[1] Not published in book form but found respectively in *Transactions of the Bristol and Gloucestershire Archaeological Society*, vol. XXXIX, 87–200, *Proceedings of the Cambridge Antiquarian Society*, vol. X, 317–360, *Derbyshire Archaeological and Natural History Society's Journal*, vol. XXXVI.

[2] Two other books, which do not deal primarily or entirely with p.n. material, call for special mention:

FÖRSTER, M. *Keltisches Wortgut im Englischen*, Halle, 1921.
RITTER, O. *Vermischte Beiträge zur Englischen Sprachgeschichte*, Halle, 1922.

ABBREVIATIONS

al.	*alias*	Nb	Northumberland
ASC	Anglo-Saxon Chronicle	NCy	North Country
BCS	Birch, *Cartularium Saxonicum*	Nf	Norfolk
		NGN	*Nomina Geographica Neerlandica*
Beds	Bedfordshire		
Berks	Berkshire	NoB	*Namn och Bygd*
Bk	Buckinghamshire	nom.	nominative
BT	Bosworth-Toller, *Anglo-Saxon Dictionary*	Norw.	Norwegian
		Nt	Nottinghamshire
C	Cambridgeshire	Nth	Northamptonshire
Ch	Cheshire	O	Oxfordshire
Co	Cornwall	ODan.	Old Danish
Cu	Cumberland	OE	Old English
D	Devonshire	OFris.	Old Frisian
Dan.	Danish	OHG	Old High German
dat.	dative	OLG	Old Low German
Db	Derbyshire	ON	Old Norse[1]
dial.	dialect(al)	OSwed.	Old Swedish
Do	Dorset	pers. name	personal name
Du	Durham	pl.	plural
E and S	*Essays and Studies*	p.n.	place-name
EDD	*English Dialect Dictionary*	PNLa	Ekwall, *Place-names of Lancashire*
ES	*Englische Studien*		
Ess	Essex	R	Rutland
Fr.	French	s.a.	sub anno
gen.	genitive	Sa	Shropshire
Germ.	German	Scand.	Scandinavian
Gl	Gloucestershire	Sc.	Scotland, Scottish
Ha	Hampshire	SCy	South Country
He	Herefordshire	Sf	Suffolk
Herts	Hertfordshire	sg.	singular
Hu	Huntingdonshire	So	Somerset
Hund	Hundred	Sr	Surrey
K	Kent	St	Staffordshire
KCD	Kemble, *Codex Diplomaticus*	St. Eng.	Standard English
		Swed.	Swedish
L	Lincolnshire	Sx	Sussex
La	Lancashire	TRE	Tempore Regis Edwardi
Lat.	Latin	TRW	Tempore Regis Willelmi
Lei	Leicestershire	W	Wiltshire
LGerm.	Low German	Wa	Warwickshire
ME	Middle English	WCy	West Country
Mod. Eng.	Modern English	We	Westmoreland
ModHG	Modern High German	Wo	Worcestershire
Mon	Monmouthshire	Wt	Isle of Wight
Mx	Middlesex	Y	Yorkshire

[1] i.e. Old Scand. generally.

PHONETIC SYMBOLS USED IN TRANSCRIPTION
OF PRONUNCIATION OF PLACE-NAMES

p	*p*ay	z	*z*one	r	*r*un	e	*r*ed
b	*b*ay	ʃ	*sh*one	l	*l*and	ei	fl*ay*
t	*t*ea	ʒ	a*z*ure	tʃ	*ch*urch	ɛː	*the*re
d	*d*ay	θ	*th*in	dʒ	*j*udge	i	p*i*t
k	*k*ey	ð	*th*en	ɑː	f*a*ther	iː	f*ee*l
g	*g*o	j	*y*ou	ɑu	c*ow*	ou	l*ow*
ʍ	*wh*en	χ	lo*ch*	ai	fl*y*	u	g*oo*d
w	*w*in	h	*h*is	æ	c*a*b	uː	r*u*le
f	*f*oe	m	*m*an	ɔ	p*o*t	ʌ	m*u*ch
v	*v*ote	n	*n*o	ɔː	s*aw*	ə	*o*ver
s	*s*ay	ŋ	si*ng*	oi	*oi*l	əː	b*i*rd

Examples:

> Harwich (**hæridʒ**), Shrewsbury (**ʃrouzbəri, ʃruːzbəri**),
> Beaulieu (**bjuːli**).

THE CHIEF ELEMENTS USED
IN ENGLISH PLACE-NAMES

IN using this list it should be noted that in giving the interpretation of any element, if that element has a direct descendant in Modern English speech, that descendant is printed in italics, e.g. **cweorn**, '*quern*, hand-mill.' Further, that where two or more p.n. are mentioned in succession and the county abbreviation is given only after one of them it is intended to apply to all the names alike. Where a p.n. occurs more than once in a county the number of times that it has been noted as occurring is expressed by the use of the necessary numeral before the county abbreviation, e.g. 2La denotes that the p.n. in question is found twice in La.

á, ON, 'river.' Greta (Cu), Rothay (We), Aby (L), E. and W. Ayton (Y). Gen. sg. *ar* in Ayresome (Y).

āc, OE, '*oak*.' Dat. pl. *æt þæm acum*, 'at the oaks,' gives Acomb (Nb, Y), Oaken (St). ME *at then oke(s)* becomes *at the noke(s)* and gives Noakes (He), Noke (O), Knockholt (K). Acton (*passim*), Aughton (Y), Aggborough, Harrock (Wo), Oxted (Sr), Occold (Sf), Othorpe (Lei), Hodsock (Nt). In Scand. districts it freely interchanges with **eik**.

ācen, OE, 'covered with *oaks*.' Akenside (Nb), Oakenrod (La). '*oaken*,' Noke Bridge (Ha).

æcer, OE, **akr**, ON, 'cultivated piece of land,' used only of arable land in OE. In Scand. districts it is impossible to distinguish the two forms. Gatacre (Sa), Linacre (La), Bessacar (Y), Alsager (Ch), Ackers (La), Uzzicar (Cu), Halnaker (Sx).

æl, OE, '*eel*.' Ely (C).

æmette, OE, '*ant*.' Ampthill (Beds).

æppel, OE, '*apple*.' Appleton (Berks), Eppleby (Y), Apperknowle (Db), Napleton (Wo). *æppeltun* is the OE term for an orchard, and must be so used in Appleton Gate in Newark (Nt) for there was never a village of Appleton. In other cases it may simply denote 'farm by (or with) an apple tree.'

ærn, OE, 'house.' Grundy has shown that this word is used to form compounds denoting a house for storing or making things. Thus we have Brewerne (Gl), Bruern (O), Cowarne (He), Colerne (= charcoal-house), Potterne (W) = pot-shed, Mixerne (Gl) = dung-house, Seasalter (K) = seasalt-house, Hordern, Hardhorn (La), Hordron (Y) = hoard-house, store-house. In Stanion (Nth) = stone-house, Askern (Y), Waldron (Sx) = forest-house, the

compounds have a different sense. Vasterne (Berks, W) seems
to be OE *fæstern*, 'stronghold.' The word is not actually found,
but it seems to lie behind the forms *fæstergeat, festergeweorc* quoted
in BT.

æsc, OE, '*ash*tree.' Ashton (*passim*), Aston in Kingsland (He),
Aisholt (So), Avenage (Gl), Hamnish (He). Nash (Gl, He, So)
shows a similar development to that given under **ac**. Esh (Du),
Eshott (Nb), Eshton (Y) show another dial. development.

æspe, æps, OE, '*aspen*.' Apsley (Wa), Aspley (Beds), Apps (Sr),
Asps (Wa). Dial. *esp* is found in Espley (Nb). ME *at ther apse* >
at the rapse and gives Rapps (So).

æspen, OE, 'grown over with *aspens*.' Aspinwall (La).

æt, OE, '*at*.' The commonest of all prepositions to be used with
p.n. As a result there arose the OE idiom of calling a place 'at X'
instead of 'X,' thus Salisbury is called *æt Searobyrg* (ASC 552), and
the stereotyped phrase of the West-Saxon royal clerks is that a
grant of land is made at the place which is called 'at X.' Hence
the numerous cases in which this preposition either as a whole or
in some shortened form, has been prefixed to a p.n. Attercliffe (Y)
is probably for *Atteclif* from *at the clif*, Thurleigh (Beds) [θəlai']
is *La Lege, Relye, Therlye* in ME documents and its varied forms
are due to misdivision of *at there lye* into *at the relye* and *at therlye*
with subsequent loss of *at*. Rivar in Ham (W) is from *at ther yver*
(v. **yfre**) and Bradley showed that the common river-name *Rea* or
Ree arose from similar misunderstanding of OE *æt þære ea*, ME *at
ther ee*, it being taken as *at the ree* (v. **ea**). Similarly Tipton (Co)
from *uptun*.

The reverse process has taken place in p.n. like Elstree (Herts),
Ickenham and Oakington (Mx), Elmsworthy (Co), all of which
once began with a *t*, which has now been absorbed by the final
t of the *at* which was so often found before them.

The common use of *at* with p.n. in the dat. case accounts for
the large number of survivals of dat. forms in p.n. See, for examples
of the sg., **burh, læs, mæd**, and of the pl., **cot, hus**.

æwiell, OE, 'river-spring.' Ewell (Ess, K, Sr), Alton (Do, Ha),
Carshalton (Sr).

æwielm, OE, *idem*. Ewelme (O), Ewen (W).

alor, OE, '*alder*.' Aller (So), Lightollers (La), Aldreth (C),
Bicknoller, Padnoller (So), Longner (Sa), Longnor (St). Gen. pl.
in Ollerton (Ch, Nt), Orleton (He, Wo), Owlerton (Y).

ān(a), OE, '*one*, lonely.' Onehouse (Sf), Onecote (St), Anston
(Y), Wanlip (Lei).

*anger, OE. The existence of this word in OE may be inferred
from Ongar (Ess), Angram (4La, Y) and, possibly, Angerton (La,
Nb). It is cognate with OHG *angar*, ModHG *anger*, 'grass-land,'

especially as opposed to forest and to arable land, but also as opposed to swampy or heath-land. *Angram* is from dat. pl. and is identical with the common Dutch p.n. *Angeren.*

ānstig, OE, lit. '*one*-path,' i.e. 'narrow path, defile' and perhaps 'stronghold,' a place which can only be approached in single file, glossed as *termofilae* and used as an alternative to **fæsten**. Fairly common as Ansty, Anstey, Anstie in the South and Midlands. The Scand. equivalent is Ainsty (Y).

apulder, apuldre, OE, '*apple*-tree.' Appledore (D, K), Apperfield (K), Appledram (Sx), Appuldercombe (Wt), Appleford (Wt).

askr, ON, 'ash-tree.' Aske (Y), Aspatria (Cu). Dat. pl. in Askam (We), Askham (La).

austr, ON, 'east.' Is fairly common in p.n. in Y and L in medieval times, but, as in Eastburn (Y), has now usually been replaced by the Eng. adj. It survives in such cases as Owston, Austwick, Owstwick (Y).

bæc, bece, OE, 'stream, brook,' ME *beche, bache.* It is specially common in Ch, Db, Sa, He, Gl, where it is used of a small valley. In *Piers Plowman* 'valeyes and hulles' of the A-text becomes 'beches and hilles' in the C-text. The word is still common in WCy dial. as *bache, bage* and *batch* and is so found in many p.n., simple and compound. The same element, with different dial. development is probably to be found in Landbeach, Waterbeach, Wisbech (C), Hackbeach (Nf), Holbeach (L), Debach (Sf). It is difficult to distinguish it from the palatalised form of the next suffix. Bache (He, Sa).

bæc, OE, **bak,** ON, '*back*,' is rare as a p.n. element. Bacup (La) shows the normal development with velar *k*. Burbage (Lei, W), earlier *Bur(h)bece*, might, so far as their form is concerned, go back to the suffix just discussed, but as both are away from valleys and streams, standing on high ground, they should probably be connected with the form *bacch* found in Orm, and explained as containing a palatalised form of *bæc*, possibly from a locative form. Such a palatalised form would explain the use of *batch* in So of the 'sandbanks or small hills lying near a river, the first rising ground above the level of the marshes.' To this also may perhaps be referred the Derbyshire *bage* used of a tract of moorland (EDD). Merbach (He) is definitely on a hill.

bǣr(e), OE, 'pasture,' especially in wooded districts, where it denoted feeding-ground for pigs. Specially common in the compounds *denbær* and *wealdbære* (v. **denn, weald**) for which the charters give the Latin alternatives *pascua* or *pastus porcorum.* As *Bere, Beer, Bear* it is common in p.n., simple and compound, in D, Do, So, Ha, Berks, but a considerable amount of confusion with **bearu** and **beorg** has taken place.

bærnet(t), OE, '*burning*,' and then applied to a place cleared by burning. Barnet (Mx, Herts), Burnett (So).

banke, ME, a common dial. word of Scand. origin denoting a ridge or shelf of ground, the slope of a hill.

bār, OE, '*boar*.' Borley (Ess), Boreham, Boarzell (Sx).

bēam, OE, 'tree' and then '*beam*.' Bempton (Y), Bampton (O), Benfleet (Ess), Holbeam (D). In p.n. it generally refers to a tree but in some, as in Bamford (La), it may refer to a 'beam.'

bēan, OE, '*bean*,' used as a first element to denote places where beans grow. Bamfurlong (La), Banstead (Sr), Binsted (Sx), Beynhurst (Berks).

bearu, OE, 'grove, wood.' The source of several places called *Barrow*. It is often difficult to distinguish them from those in which *barrow* is derived from **beorg**. Still in dial. use in Du and Ch to denote 'copse, thicket, dingle.' Sedgeberrow (Wo).

bēce, OE, '*beech*.' Beech (Sr), Cowbeech (Sx).

bedd, OE, '*bed*, place where plants grow.' Nettlebed (O).

bēger, OE, 'berry.' Barmoor (Nb), Byermoor (Du), Bairstow (Y).

bekkr, ON, 'stream, *beck*.' Common throughout the North of England (with the exception of Nb) and the Danelaw generally. As the word is in common dial. use in these districts, it is no definite proof of Scand. settlement. Thus in Du it has often taken the place of *burn*, the only form found in early documents. Gen. sg. *bekkjar* in Beckermet (Cu), Beckermonds (Y). *Beck-* at the beginning of names is usually from a pers. name *Becca*.

bēo, OE, '*bee*.' Beoley (Wo), Beal (Nb), Beauworth (Ha).

beofor, OE, '*beaver*.' Bevere, Barbourne (Wo).

bēonet, OE, found only in p.n. such as *beonetleah*. Late ME *bent* is used of long coarse grass or rushes, especially on moorland and near the sea, and a similar use is found in dial. That is its sense in Bentley (*passim*), Bentham (Gl, Y). The word is also used derivatively of open grassland as opposed to woodland, and of sandy hillocks covered with 'bents.' So in Chowbent (La), Totley Bents (Db).

beorc, OE, 'birch-tree.' Barkham (Berks), Berkeley (Gl), Barford (Beds). Whether spelt *Berk-* or *Bark-*, it is to be pronounced as [ba·k].

beorg, OE, 'hill,' whether natural or artificial. The former sense survives in dial. *barf*, 'low ridge or hill' (Y, L) and *barrow* used of a long low hill in Cu, La. In the South and South-west *barrow* is, and probably always has been, more generally used to denote an artificial hill, a 'barrow' in the archaeological sense of the term. In p.n. in Scand. England it is very difficult to distinguish it from ON **berg** but it should be noted that the latter term was not used of a barrow in the technical sense. It assumes a wide variety of forms in p.n., partly because the nom. and dat. sg. *beorg* and *beorge* become *berg(h)* and *berwe* respectively, while these again may show the common change of *er* to *ar*, giving *barg(h)* and *barwe*. Thus we get *Berrow* and *Barrow*. Further the suffix had in later times been completely confused with **burh** and *byrig* (dat. sg.) so that all over the South and Midlands it appears again and again as *-borough* and *-burgh* and even as *-bury*. Barham (C), Burford (O), Burghfield (Berks), Broughton (L), Berkhamstead (Herts), Whinburgh (Nf), Sharperton (Nb).

beorht, OE, 'shining, clear, *bright*.' Brightwell (O), Birtley (Du). In BCS 830 *beorhtan wille* is translated *declaratam fontem*.

bere, OE, 'barley, *bere* (dial.)' as in Baracre (K) and **beretun** and **berewic**.

bere-tūn, OE, literally 'barley-farm' (v. **tun**), but used in the Middle Ages in a special sense to denote a 'grange situated in an outlying part of a manor, where the lord's crop was stored.' The term is found in place-names all over England but only remains in living use in the South and South-West, where it denotes either (1) a farm- or rick-yard, or (2) a grange of the type just described. In Devonshire it is commonly added to a parish name to denote the manor-farm of the parish, e.g. Sampford Barton. The early forms of some of the *Bartons* compel us to postulate an OE *bær-tun* side by side with *bere-tun*, containing an alternative form of the word for barley. Cf. OE *bærlic*, 'barley.'

bere-wīc, OE, lit. 'barley-wick' (v. **wic**), but used already in the tenth century to denote an outlying portion of an estate. In this sense it forms the 'berewick' of Domesday, a tenement or group of tenements in the hands of the lord, but lying apart from the manorial centre. It usually appears as Berwick but it is also found as Barwick (Y) and Borwick (La).

berg, ON, 'hill.' The source of many p.n. in *-ber(gh)* and *-barrow* in Cu, We, La, Y and also in *-borough* as noted under **beorg**, e.g. Breckenborough (Y). The modern form *-ber* as in Hoober (Y), Kaber (We) seems often to go back to the Scand. word. In all other cases it is difficult to decide whether we have the Eng. or the Scand. word, unless the first element is also distinctively Scand. as in Aigburth (La).

berige, OE, '*berry*.' Bericote (Wa).

bern, OE, '*barn*,' often found in the pl. Berne (Do), Barnes (Sr), Whitburn (Du).

bierce, OE, '*birch*,' *birk* in NCy, when it is very difficult to distinguish from ON **birki**. Burcher (He).

biercen, 'overgrown with *birches*.' Birkenside (Nb).

bī(g), OE, '*by*.' Found in a good many p.n., the settlement having taken its name from its nearness to some prominent object. Biford (Gl), Bygrave (Herts), Byfield (Nth), Byfleet (Sr), Bythorne (Hu), Byker, Bywell (Nb), Beeleigh (Ess).

bigging, ME, 'building, dwelling-place, *biggin*.' A word in common dial. use formed from a Scand. vb. and no definite criterion of Scand. settlement.

bi(o)nnan, OE, 'within.' Is found as the first element in certain p.n. but it is not always easy to distinguish it from the pers. name *Bynna* or *Bynni*. St Mary Bynnewerk in Stamford (L), Binney in Canterbury (K), from *binnan ea*, rendered *inter duos rivos gremiales fluminis* (BCS 344), Benwell (Nb), where *well* is for *wall*.

birki, ON, 'place grown over with birch, birch-copse.' Birkland (Nt), Birthwaite (Y), Burthwaite (We), Briscoe (Cu, Y), Busco (Y).

biscop, OE, '*bishop*,' common in names of places which were once in episcopal possession. Found in Bishton (Sa, St), Bispham (La), Biscathorpe (L) and, with the dial. development which gave the fairly common early Mod. Eng. *bushoppe*, in Bushwood (Wa), Bushbury (St), Bushton (W).

blāc, OE, 'pale, white' and

blæc, OE, '*black*,' are often very difficult to distinguish owing to the shortening of vowel which the former may undergo in a compound before a consonant-group. The latter is found in Blaxton (Y), Blagdon (Nb, So), Blagrove (Berks).

blár, ON, 'dark, blue, livid,' surviving in NCy *bloa*, *blae*, 'livid, leaden, cheerless, cold, exposed.' Blaby (L), Blea Tarn (We), Blowick (La). Cognate with

* **blā(w)**, OE, which we find in Blofield (Nf).

bleikr, ON, 'pale, livid,' dial. *blake* is used similarly. It is difficult in NCy to distinguish it from its Eng. cognate *blake* from **blac** and from the nickname *Bleik*, *Blake* to which it gave rise. Blaithwaite (Cu).

bōc, OE, 'beech,' found as the first element in p.n., generally with shortened vowel, as *Bock-* or, more usually, as *Buck-*. Buckhurst (*passim*), Bockhampton (Do). It is often very difficult to distinguish it from the pers. name *Bucca* and the common animal names **bucc** and **bucca**. Boughton (K).

* **bōcen**, OE, 'beechen, overgrown with beeches.' Bockenfield (Nb) and probably Bochidene (Wa). Almost impossible in ME to distinguish from *bukken*, gen. sg. of **bucca**. Probably found in a few such names as Bucknell (O), Buckenhill (He). *bōcen* is not found in OE, the form there being *bēcen*, but we may assume a double form as in **acen** and **ǣcen**.

bōcland, OE, lit. '*book*-land,' but used in the technical sense of land granted by *boc* or charter, or, more strictly, 'land over which certain rights and privileges were granted by charter.' In Latin versions of the OE laws it is variously rendered as *terra testamentalis, libera terra, terra hereditatis, feudum*. It is the source of the numerous Bucklands in England but the furthest north of these is in Mid. Lincolnshire. It is just possible that *boc* in this sense may enter into some other p.n. compounds (cf. OE *bocæceras*, meaning apparently 'fields granted by *boc*'), but it is impossible from the form alone to distinguish these compounds from those formed with *boc*, 'beech-tree.'

bóndi, ON. In Iceland this term denoted a peasant proprietor and it was an honourable one. In Norway and Denmark it came to have a less honourable sense and denoted the common people. At the time that the term was introduced into England it was still used in the earlier sense and was the equivalent of OE **ceorl**. In later times it was used of unfree tenants but the p.n. compounds in which it is found were probably of early formation and one may therefore assume the earlier sense. Thus it is the first element in Bonby (L), which was held TRE by six *taini*, the tenure probably giving rise to the name. Burstwick (Y), earlier *Bondburstwick*, took its name from the *bonde* who, as late as 1297, still held certain lands in the village from the king. Bomby (We), Bonbusk (Nt).

borg, ON, 'fort, fortified hill.' Borrowdale (Cu, We).

bōþ, ODan., **búð**, ON, '*booth*, temporary shelter.' Still in dial. use, meaning 'cowhouse' (La, Y), 'herdsman's hut' (La), 'outlying hamlet' (L). In England, as in Scandinavia, the term is usually found in the pl. The nom. pl. is found in Butterilket, the gen. sg. in Bowderdale (Cu), the dat. pl. in Bootham (Y).

The two forms give respectively *bothe* and *bouthe* in ME. In Mod. Eng. the Dan. form has usually ousted the Norse but Ekwall notes Bouth (2) and Rulbuth (La). Boothby (L), Scorbrough (Y).

***bōðl, bold, bōtl**, OE, 'building,' but used both of an ordinary house and also of monastic buildings and of a manor-house. After the Conquest the phrase *capitale mesuagium* corresponds to OE *heafod-botl* and means 'manor-house.' Ekwall has a full discussion of these forms and their distribution in *Anglia Beiblatt*, 28, 82 ff. From them we get several names in *-bottle* in Nb and Du, one in Nth (Nobottle Grove), Bootle (Cu, La) and several p.n. in *-bo(u)ld*, both simple and compound, in the Central and West Midlands. Not found in Wessex, Southern and South-Eastern England or in East Anglia.

***bōðltun**, OE, compound of **boðl** and **tun** lies behind the numerous Boltons in Nb, Du, Cu, We, La, Y and seems to be confined to these counties and South Scotland. Ekwall suggests very plausibly (PNLa) that the term had some special technical sense and compares OSwed. *bolbyr*, a compound whose first element is cognate with *boðl*, and which is used of the 'village proper' in contrast to the surrounding outlying land.

botm, OE, **botn**, ON, '*bottom*,' used in p.n. of the lowest part of a valley or of an alluvial hollow. Starbottom (Y), Wythburn (Cu), Botton (La).

box, OE, '*box*-tree.' Boxford (Berks).

brād, OE, '*broad*.' Very common in p.n. and usually found with shortened vowel before a following consonant-group, as in the numerous Bradfields, Bradleys, Bradfords and Bradwells. Forms with *Broad*- are modern, or modern re-spellings due to the influence of the independent word. Bredgar (K). The weak dat. sg. *bradan* has given rise to Bradiford (D), Bradenham (Bk).

bræc, brec, OE, dial. *brack, breck*, 'strip of uncultivated land,' 'strip of land taken in from a forest by royal licence, for temporary cultivation.' Difficult in Scand. England to distinguish from **brekka**. Braxted (Ess).

brǣr, OE, 'thorn-bush, *briar*,' of wider application than the modern word. Its normal development is to ME *brere*, which survives in common dial. [bri·ə] and in such p.n. as Brereton (Ch), Brearton (Du). In others it has been replaced, at least in spelling, by the form *brier* which arose in the 16th cent., e.g. Brierley (St). Brierden (Nb) has the new spelling but the old pronunciation. Briestwistle (Y).

braken, ME, '*bracken*,' is allied to Dan. *bregne*, Swed. *bräken*, 'fern,' and its distribution in p.n. confirms its Scand. origin. Bracondale, Bracon Ash (Nf), Breckenborough (Y).

brame, ME, 'brier, bramble,' still used in dialect. Bramham (Y), Brampton (Hu). The wide use of the term in p.n. suggests that this word, not recorded in OE, goes back far earlier than the earliest dictionary record in 1425. Brampton (Hu) is *Bramtun* in 1121 (ASC *s.a.*).

brant, bront, OE, 'steep,' ME *brant, brent*. In many cases we may have the cognate ON *brattr*, earlier *brant*, cf. Swed. *brant*. Brantbeck (La), Brincliffe (Y), Bransty (Cu).

breiðr, ON, 'broad.' Braithwell, Braworth, Brayton (Y), Bratoft (L), Brathay (We).

brekka, ON, 'slope, hill.' Distinctively West Scand. Breck, Sunbrick, Larbrick (La), Haverbrack (We). It is often difficult to distinguish it from **bræc**.

brēmel, brǣmel, bræmbel, brembel, OE, '*bramble*.' Used by itself, as in Bremhill (W), or compounded, as in Bramshott (Ha), Bremilham (W).

brende, brente, ME, 'burnt,' as in Brandwood (La), Brentwood (Ess), Brent Pelham (Herts). In compounds with wood its meaning is clear. In other cases it probably refers to some fire in the past history of these places. It is not always easy to distinguish this element from *brant*.

bridd, OE, 'young *bird*.' Birdham (Sx).

brinke, brenke, ME, '*brink*, edge of a steep place, edge of land bordering on water.' It is the East Scand. equivalent (cf. Dan. *brink*) of the Norse *brekka*. As the first element in p.n. it cannot be assumed, except possibly in names of demonstrably late origin, in parts of England not subject to Scand. influence. In all cases when it is used as the first element in a p.n. it is difficult to distinguish it from the OE pers. name *Brynca*. Micklebring (Y).

brōc, OE, '*brook*,' but used also in K and Sx of a water-meadow or low marshy ground (EDD), a sense which is found also in the cognate Germ. *bruch*, LGerm. *brok*. Not found in p.n. in Nb or Du, little used in the North and East Ridings of Y and very rare in East Anglia. It is often compounded with **tun** giving rise to numerous Broughtons, Brocktons, Broctons and to Bratton (Sa), Brotton (Y). Here and elsewhere it is often difficult to know if we have this word, with shortening of the long vowel in the compound, or

brocc, OE, *brock*, 'badger.' Further possibility of confusion with *brocc* used as a pers. name has been suggested but, at least so far as p.n. of English origin are concerned, there is little likelihood of this. Broxbourne (Herts), Browston (Sf), Broxted (Ess).

brocc-hol, 'badger-hole.' Brockhale, Brocklehurst (La), Brockhill (Wo), Brockle (Co), Brockholds (Ess), Brockhall (Nth).

brōm, OE, '*broom*.' Common by itself and in compounds. The forms in ME often show confusion with **brame**. Brimfield (He), Brimrod (La).

brōmig, 'covered with *broom*.' Broomy Holm (Du), Brimmicroft (La).

brūn, OE, '*brown*.' Burnmoor (Y).

brunnr, ON, 'spring,' is very difficult to distinguish from its English cognate **burna**, for each may undergo metathesis of the *r* and then the Norse word resembles the English and *vice-versa*. Barbon (We).

brycg, OE, '*bridge*,' commonly found either in that form or in the NCy *brig*(g) but in the majority of p.n. the latter form has been ousted by the St. Eng. one. The form *brugge* is common in the South and South-West in ME but has usually been replaced by the St. Eng. one in present-day nomenclature. It survives in Brushford (D). Doveridge (Db).

bucc, OE, '*buck*' and **bucca**, 'he-goat,' but it is practically impossible to distinguish these animal-names from the pers. name *Bucca*.

bufan, OE, '*above*.' This preposition is sometimes compounded
with the noun which it once governed but it is difficult to distinguish it from the pers. name *Bofa*. Boveridge, Bucknowl (Do),
Bowlhead (Sr) may contain it.

*bula, OE, '*bull*,' is not found in OE but it is so common in
OE p.n. that we must assume its use and can hardly think of
it as a Scand. loan-word. At times it may be a pers. name.
Bulmer (Ess, Nb), Bolney (Sx), Bulstrode (Bk), Bowforth (Y).

būr, OE, '*bower*.' In OE it is chiefly used in poetry. In glossaries
it is found as the equivalent of *camera* and *cubiculum*. At times
it seems to be used for a house or room, e.g. the Bishop's house at
Worcester (KCD 2, 100) or a room in an Ealdorman's (ASC 1015).
In p.n. it is almost invariably used in an uncompounded form and
then often in the plural. Bower (D), Bure (Ha), Bures (Sf), Bowers
Gifford (Ess).

burh, OE, dat. sg. **byrig**, is very common in p.n. When used by
itself or as a suffix it takes various forms. If the nom. form survives we may have *borough, burgh, brough, burrough, borrow*, while
the dat. appears as *bury* or *berry*. As the first element in a p.n.
it is naturally the nom. form alone which is found, as in Burwell
(C), Burbage (Lei, W), Burradon (Nb), Borley (Wo), Bearley (Wa)
and the various descendants of **burhtun**.

The primary sense of *burh* is 'fortified place' and the term was
applied by our forefathers to Roman or pre-historic defensive
works, earthworks and the like, as well as to their own forts.
This is certainly its sense in the great majority of those p.n. in
which it forms the first element and probably in the great majority
of the others as well. The former class should for the most part be
interpreted as denoting places near some old *burh*, rather than as
places which were themselves actually fortified, thus Burwell is
the 'spring by the *burh*' rather than the 'fortified spring.'

From this primary sense various other uses developed. The
word is used of a fortified house. It was also used of such towns
and other places as were fortified as part of a national scheme of
defence. Without a knowledge of the past history of a place, such as
we do not usually possess, it is impossible to say how far one or other
of these meanings may lie behind the element *burh* when found in
its name. Occasionally we have the historical evidence which will
settle the question. Hertingfordbury (Herts) is one of the two forts
built by Edward the Elder at Hertford in 913 as part of his scheme
of defence against the Danes (ASC *s.a.*). Burpham (Sx) is a *burh*
in the Burghal Hidage and goes back to the same reign. In Bury
St Edmunds and Peterborough we know that the element is of
comparatively late origin, the earlier names of these places having
been respectively, *Beadoricesuuyrthe* and *Medeshamstede*. It was

only when these settlements had become towns of some importance that they came to be known as the 'burhs' of St Edmund and St Peter, and *burh* would seem to denote 'town' in contrast to the original small village or hamlet. Newbrough (Nb) on the other hand is of quite different and still later origin. It is the *novus burgus* in the manor of Thornton-in-Tynedale which took its rise from the grant of a market in 1221 (Hodgson, *History of Nb*, 2. 3. 391). Similarly Newbury (Berks) first appears in the early 12th century and was undoubtedly a new market-town created by Ernulf de Hesdinc for the benefit of his tenants.

There is one further type of name formed with this element. From the old use of *burh* to denote a fortified house, there arose the use of *bury* for a 'court or manor-house, the centre of a *soke* or other jurisdiction.' Such names are all of post-Conquest origin and first become common in the 13th century. They are almost entirely confined to Mx, Herts, Ess, Bk. They are most familiar in the London Bloomsbury, Lothbury and the like, but other examples are Flamstead Bury (Herts), Bassettsbury (Bk).

In modern p.n. much confusion with **beorg** has taken place, as in Burghfield (Berks), and it is only in the North and North Midlands that names which now end in *-burgh, -borough* go back at all commonly to *burh*.

In the Southern Danelaw, more especially in Nth and Lei, this suffix in Domesday often alternates with **by** and there can be little doubt that many of the p.n. which now end in *-by* once had the suffix *byrig*. A good early example is Badby (Nth) which in the same charter (BCS 792), an original document dated 944, is called both *Baddanby* and *Baddanbyrig*.

burhsteall = **burh** + **steall**, OE, i.e. site of a *burh*, as in Birstal (Lei), Birstall (Y), Burstall (Sf), Boarstall (Bk). In Borstal (2K) we may have a different word. Borstal in Rochester is *borhsteall* in the 10th century endorsement of a charter (BCS 339) while from Sx we have the form *Gealtborgsteal*. These forms would seem to go with the K and Sx dial. use of *borstal* to denote 'pathway up a steep hill.' Form and meaning alike suggest association with *borg*, 'surety' or **beorg** rather than *burh*, though *borg* cannot have come directly from *beorg*. Perhaps it is simply a case of confusion of two words, for *burhsteal* is found in an OE vocabulary glossed as *clivus* or *discensus*, and is thus given the sense of *borgsteall*. *Burhsteall* has its parallel in Germ. *borstel*, fairly common as a p.n. in Hanover and Holstein.

burhstede = **burh** + **stede**, OE, apparently the same as **burhsteall**. Burstead (Ess).

burhtun, OE, a very common compound of **burh** and **tun**, not found in OE, apart from p.n., except in the *Wife's Complaint*, where it is used in the pl., and the wife, speaking of her place of exile, says that 'the *burgtunas* are overgrown with briers, the dwellings (**wic**) are joyless.' This would seem to refer to the *tun* or enclosure round a *burh* or fortified house and that is probably the sense of the term in most p.n., viz. that it describes an enclosed settlement with a *burh* as its nucleus. If the name is in any case of definitely later origin it might simply mean 'settlement or farm near a *burh*,' whether earthwork or fortified house. It commonly takes the form *Burton* in later times but we also have it as Bourton (Berks), Broughton (Nth), Boreton (Sa).

burna, OE, 'stream, *burn*,' is in common use for a stream throughout England. Occasionally it undergoes metathesis of the *r* as in Brunton (Nb). Still in common dial. use in Nb and Du.

buskr, ON, 'bush.' Bonbusk (Nt), Busby (Y).

butere, OE, '*butter*,' is often compounded with *worth*, *wick*, *ley* and other suffixes and is descriptive of a settlement with good pasture. Butterleigh (D), Birley (He), Bitterley (Sa).

Late OE **by** from ON *býr*, *bær*, Swed., Dan. *by*. The word in Icelandic denoted a 'farm' or 'landed estate,' but in Norse, Swedish, and Danish it has come to be used of a town or village. The suffix is so common in p.n. in Scand. England, and is applied to so many places that can never have been more than a farmstead or at most a hamlet, that it would be unsafe to render it always by 'town' or 'village.' Further evidence of this is found in the gloss in the Lindisfarne Gospels (c. 950) where the unclean spirit dwells in *hus* vel *lytelo by*. The term was in independent use in Northern dialect in ME so that it is not always safe to assume that a place whose name ends in -*by* was actually settled by Scandinavians and there are cases of p.n. in *by* containing Norman pers. names, e.g. Aglionby (Cu). There are a good many cases in Domesday of this suffix alternating with *birie* from *byrig* (cf. **burh**). The gen. sg. was *byjar* and is found in Birstwith (Y) and (Birstath) Bryning (La) where it is compounded with **staðr** and also in

*býjarlǫg, ON, 'law(s) of a *by* or township' and also 'district over which the *by*-laws held good.' The term is not actually found in ON but has its parallel in Swed. *byalag*, 'village community,' and must lie behind the common *birlag*, *birlawe* of medieval times and the Bierlow of several Yorkshire p.n., such as Ecclesall Bierlow.

bygg, ON, 'barley, *bigg* (dial.).' Bigland (La).

byht, OE, '*bight*, bend, curve.' Sidebeet (La), Bight in streetnames in Lincoln.

býre, OE, '*byre*, shed, hovel.' In independent use, often in the pl., as in Byers Green (Du) and in compounds such as Burton

Joyce (Nt), Burton-on-Trent (St), Burland, Burstall Lane (Y), Edmundbyers (Du). Dat. pl. in Byram (Y).

*bysc, OE, 'bush, thicket,' assumed by Skeat to explain the various ME forms *bisshe, busshe, bysshe* found in p.n. These could not all go back to an anglicised version of ON *buskr*, hitherto taken to be the source of English *bush*. Bushey (Herts), Bushley (Wo), Bysshe Court (Sr).

*byxe, OE, 'box-tree' or perhaps rather 'box-thicket.' Such a derivative of *box* may be assumed on the analogy of **þorn, þyrne** and is needed to explain the forms of such names as Bix (O), Bexhill (Sx) and Bexley (K).

cærse, cerse, cresse, OE, '*cress*,' is very common in compounds with **wielle**. It develops a wide variety of forms in later times as in Kerswell (D), Carswell (Gl), Caswell (O, So), Craswall (He), Cresswell (St), Carshalton (Sr). A similar compound with **kelda** is found in Kirskill *alias* Creskeld (Y).

calc, cealc, OE, 'chalk.' The relation of these forms is the same as that of **cald, ceald**, *infra*, and is reflected in the difference between such p.n. as Chalk (K, W), Chalton (Beds, Ha), Chalford (Gl), on the one hand, and Cawkwell (L), on the other.

cald, ceald, OE, '*cold*.' The first form belongs to Anglian, the second to Kentish and Saxon England. The former gives *cald*, later *cold*, in ME but in p.n. the vowel has usually undergone shortening, so that we get initial *Cald-* in p.n. while association with the independent adj. *cold* has often led to the substitution of that form for the more correct *Cald-*, as in Coldwell (Nb). The latter form gives *Chald-*, as in Chaldwell (Do), Chadwell (Ess), Chalfield (W). There has however been a good deal of replacing of the Southern *Chald-* under the influence of Midland (i.e. St Eng.) forms in *Cald-*, especially in p.n. in which the sense association with the common adj. was readily apparent. Thus *Caldecote*, with its variants *Calcott, Caulcott*, has entirely replaced forms with initial *ch*. In So, D, Co we get, as in Chold Ash (D), a curious form which seems to result from *ceald > chāld > chōld*. (See Ekwall, *Contrib. to the Hist. of OE Dialects*, 1–39.) Challacombe (D), Cholwell (So), Goldicote (Wo).

calf, cealf, celf, OE, '*calf*.' This shows the same dial. history as **cald**. Many p.n. show the gen. pl. *cealfra* or *cealfa* rather than the nom. sg. Chaldon (Do, Sr), Chalvey (Bk), Challock (K), Cholswell (Berks), Cawston (Wa), Cawton (Y), Kelloe (Du), Chelvey (So), Kellah (Nb). Gen. pl. in Callerton (Nb), Calverton (Bk, Nt).

calu, OE, 'bald, bare.' Callaughton (Sa), Cow Honeyburn (Gl), Callaly (Nb), Calverley (D).

camb, OE, '*comb*,' then used of a crest and so of a crest or ridge of land. No example of this last sense-development is found in

OE but it is clearly evidenced in ME and has given rise to NCy and Sc *kame, kaim,* 'long narrow ridge or hill.' Combs (Sf), Cam (Y).

camp, comp, OE, as a p.n. term is only found in charter material. It is an old Teutonic loan-word from the Latin *campus.* That it could denote an enclosed area in OE seems to be clear from the expression *campæs geat* (BCS 758). For further light on its meaning we may perhaps turn to its Continental cognates. In OLG and in OFris., *kamp* denotes an enclosed piece of land. In West Hanover it denotes 'a large area of arable land in the neighbourhood of the farm-house' (Middendorff). Jellinghaus (*Die West-fälischen Ortsnamen,* 83–4) says that the term is almost entirely Saxon and Frisian and is used of enclosed land whether arable or pasture or wood-land. See also NGN iii, 342. The term is not in living use in English, and in p.n. it has as a rule been confused with some other suffix, generally *combe,* as in Swanscombe (K), Sacombe (Herts), Ruscombe (Berks), Barcombe (Sx), Bossingham (K), Bulcamp (Sf), Shudy and Castle Camps (C), Chipping Campden (Gl), though in this last name we may have *camp* in its other sense of 'battle, war, contest.' The examples illustrate the somewhat narrow distribution of this suffix.

carr, OE, 'rock,' only found in Northumbrian OE. Carham (Nb) is from the dat. pl.

catt, catte, OE, doubtless occurs in p.n. but it is impossible to distinguish it from pers. names of similar form.

cēap, OE, 'market.' Chepstow (Mon), Chipstead (K, Sr).

ceart, cert, OE, is only found in charter material but it may be assumed to have had the same meaning as dial. *chart* (K, Sr), viz. 'a rough common, overgrown with gorse, broom, bracken' (EDD). Each settlement will have had its 'chart' in certain parts of those counties and it will originally have been forest-land which was later absorbed as the settlers spread themselves. Thus we hear of Kemsing's *ceart* (BCS 370) and to this day we have names like Seal Chart and Chart Sutton. These 'charts' are found in the greensand and Weald clay districts. Other examples are Chartham (K) and Churt (Sr). It is doubtful if the term is found outside these counties.

ceaster, cæster, OE. A loan-word from the Lat. *castra,* 'camp' and used independently in OE to denote a large city or town. It may have this sense in the names of some of the towns and cities famous in Roman times, as in Gloucester, Chester, Bath (earlier *Baþanceaster*), but its wide use in p.n. and the size and character of many of the places, indeed the great proportion of them, show that there it is used of any site whatever on which fortifications of any kind, or the remains of such, were to be found. There is no doubt also that the term is applied to sites in which the defensive works were of pre-Roman origin. Our forefathers were not archaeologists.

By itself, and as prefix and suffix, this element takes three definite forms. The commonest is *chester*, the other two are *cester* and *caster*, with variants Castor (Nth) and Caistor (L, 2Nf). The form *cester* slightly disguised in Craster (Nb), Mancetter (Wa), Exeter (D), Wroxeter (Sa), is due to Anglo-Norman influence upon English spelling and pronunciation, and its distribution need not be discussed. *chester* is found in Nb, Du, La (S. of the Ribble), Ch, St, Db, Wa, He, Gl, O, So, D, Do, Ha, Sx, K, Ess, Herts, C, Hu and one example in South Nth. *caster* is found in Y, La (N. of the Ribble), Cu (in the form *castle*), We, L, Nf, R, Nth (one in the North). Two explanations of this distribution have been offered. The first is that the *caster* forms are due to Scand. influence and it cannot be denied that the *caster* forms are found in just the right places to fit this theory but there are grave difficulties in accepting it. If *caster* forms are due to the well recognised substitution of Scand. *k* for English *ch*, as in Yorkshire *Skyrack* for *scirac*, 'shire-oak,' then we should expect two things, viz. (i) that the form in ME would be *kester* rather than *caster*, (ii) that at least a few stray *chester* forms would have survived unchanged, but such is not the case. The difference is rather to be sought, as Ekwall (*Anglia Beiblatt*, 30, 224–5) has shown, in differences between Northern and Eastern and Southern and Western dialects, the palatalisation and assibilation of initial *c* never having been completely carried through in the former. Nb and Du in this word and others with initial *c* hold a peculiar position which has yet fully to be explained. Bewcastle (Cu), Castleford (Y), Cheshunt (Herts), Cester Over (Wa).

celde, OE, 'spring,' only found in charter material, the Eng. equivalent of ON **kelda**. Honeychild, Bapchild (K), Absoll Park (Ess).

ceorl, OE, 'peasant, rustic,' contrasted with the *eorl* on the one hand, who was of noble birth, and with the *þeow*, who was a slave, on the other. In place-names it is commonest in the Charltons and Chorltons found throughout the country, as also in Charaton (Co), which go back to OE *ceorla tun*, 'farm of the ceorls.' It is difficult to determine the precise sense of this compound. Is it simply, where the churls live, or has it some more technical sense? Found also in Chorley (La), Cherubeer (Co), Chalgrave (O), Churlwell (Y). It is noteworthy that this element *ceorla* (gen. pl.) is not found in compounds with **ham** and **burh**—Charlbury (O) is misleading—and probably not with **worþ**. In Chelsworth (Sf), Cholstrey (He) we probably have the singular *Ceorl*, used as a pers. name.

ceosol, cisel, OE, 'gravel, shingle.' Cf. Chesil Bank. Chesilborne (Do), Chiselhurst (K), Chillesford (Sf).

cīeping, OE, 'market,' found in a good many p.n. of the type Chipping Ongar (Ess) and denoting a place with a market.

cīese, OE, '*cheese*,' used like **butere** to denote a good cheese-making farm. Chiswick (Ess), Cheswick (Nb), Cheswardine (Sa). It is often difficult to distinguish it from **cis** and from the pers. name *Cissa*. In Scand. Eng. it is Scandinavianised to *Kes*- in Keswick (Cu, Nf, Y).

cietel, OE, 'kettle' is found in OE in the compounds *cytelwylle* (BCS 610) and *cytelflod* (ib. 682), where it must describe a 'bubbling' spring or stream. The former has survived in Chitterwell (So). In such p.n. as Chattlehope (Nb) it seems to describe the shape of a valley. The Scand. cognate is probably found in Kettlewell (Y) but it is difficult to be sure in many of these names whether we may not have the pers. names which have given us later *Chettle* and *Kettle*.

cild, OE. This word, the ancestor of *child*, enters into a good many p.n. as the first element. Found as a rule in the gen. pl. form *cilda* or *cildra*, as in *cilda stan* (BCS 667), *cylda tun* (ib. 565) and Childerley (C). It is found in most of the Chiltons and Chilcotes and in Child Hanley (St). Its exact sense is uncertain. The sg. is used as a title of honour in late OE times and this is found also throughout the Middle Ages, as in '*Childe* Roland.' Of the social status of the 'children' who gave their name to certain places we know nothing definite. They were not children in the modern sense of the term and possibly a ray of light may be thrown on their status by the fact that Childerley, TRE, was held by 4 *Sochemanni*.

cirice, OE, **kirkja**, ON, '*church*.' In Northern England it is often impossible to tell whether we have a Northern form *kirk* of the OE word or the Scand. loan-word. In p.n. too one has to distinguish this element very carefully from that found in Kirkley (Nb), Crich (Db), Crick (Nth), Crichel (Do), Creech (So), Croichlow (La), Crickley (Gl) and numerous other p.n. such as Woodcray (Berks). The clue to these names is to be found in an OE charter (BCS 62) in which a grant is made on the Tone (OE *Tan*) near the hill *qui dicitur brittanica lingua Cructan apud nos Crycbeorh*. This is the modern Creech St Michael (So) and in another charter (BCS 550) the same place is apparently called *cyricestun*, i.e. farm of the *cyric*. This British *cruc*, OE *cryc*, (?) *cyric*, is the same as the Irish *cruach*, Welsh *crug*, Cornish, Breton *cruc*, 'hill, barrow.' It is noteworthy that the English in taking it over frequently added their own word to the name, thus **beorh** in *crycbeorh*, **hlaw** in Kirkley (Nb), Croichlow (La), **hyll** in Crichel. Further topographical investigation is needed but we may note that there are such 'hills, motehills' or 'barrows' at Crich, Crick, Kirkley, Woodcray, Crickley and probably at all the others as well. Barrows, unluckily, may have disappeared. If *Pennocrucium* in the Antonine Itinerary is to be identified with Penkridge (St), *Pencric* in BCS 1317, we have a Latin transcription of this British word. The change of vowel from *u* to OE *y*, *i* is explained by the fact that already in the 7th century *u* in British approached an *i*-sound. (Cf. Strachan, *Introd. to Early Welsh*, p. 1.)

*cis, OE, 'gravel,' is not actually recorded in OE but seems to be found in the p.n. *cisburna* (BCS 356) and in certain other names surviving in later forms, such as Chesham, Cheesden (La), Chishall (Ess), while the deriv. adj. *cisen* would account for Chisnall (La). It is the stem from which **ceosol** is derived.

clæfer, OE, '*clover*.' Claverley (Sa), Clarborough (Nt), Clarewood (Nb).

clæg, OE, '*clay*.' Clayhanger (Ess), Clehonger (He), Clinger (Gl), Cley (Nf), Clare (O).

clægig, '*clayey*.' Claydon (O, Sf).

clæne, OE, '*clean*, clear of weeds or other hurtful growth.' In the OE trans. of the *Cura Pastoralis* the Lat. *terra quae nullas spinas habuit* is rendered by *clæne land*. Clanfield (Ha, O), Clennell (Nb), Glendon (Nth), Glenfield (Lei), Glanville (D).

clāte, OE, '*clote*, burdock.' Clatworthy (So), Clatford (W).

clif, OE, '*cliff*,' but in OE, as in modern local usage, it was not confined to a 'steep face of rock, a precipitous declivity.' In D the form *cleve* (v. *infra*) is used of the steep side of a hill, any steep sloping ground, while in L, the 'Cliff' is the name now given to the sloping and cultivated escarpment of the oolite which runs down the county from the Humber to Lincoln. The topography of many places whose name ends in *clif* shows that it cannot there be used in the modern St. Eng. sense.

Final *f* is often lost (cf. Fr. *joli* from *jolif*) and the suffix is then assimilated to *ley*, as in Hockley (Beds). OE *clif* had a pl. *clifu* or *cleofu* and from the latter, or from the fresh singular *cleof* made to fit it, come the forms *cle(e)ve* found in dial. and in p.n. Cleveland (Y), Cleadon (Du), Clevedon, Clewer (So), Clee (He), Cleobury (Sa), Clibburn (We).

clōh, OE, '*clough*, ravine,' is still in common dial. use in the North and N.W. Midlands. The common dial. pron. is [kluf] or [klau]. Catcleugh (Nb), Cowclough (La), Haltcliff (Cu).

cnæpp, OE, 'top, summit of a hill, short sharp ascent.' In p.n. in Scand. England it is difficult to distinguish from ON *knappr*. Knapp (So), Knepp (Sx).

cniht, OE, 'boy, youth, servant' and then 'servant of some military superior such as the king.' It is our *knight* but in OE, usage and in p.n. had not got beyond the stages just given. Common in various Knightons, Knightcotes and Knightleys. Its exact sense in such names, where it represents OE *cnihta* (gen. pl.), is uncertain, but we may note that Knighton (Berks) was held by 5 *liberi homines*, (Do) by 2 *taini*, (Ha) by 8 *liberi homines*, all TRE.

cnoll, OE, '*knoll*,' but used in earlier times of the rounded top of a larger hill and not confined as now to a hillock or mound. Knole (K), Knowle (So), Chipnall (Sa).

cocc, OE, '*cock*.' Doubtless found in a good many names but difficult to distinguish from the OE pers. name *Cocc(a)*.

cofa, OE, '*cove*.' Its sense in p.n. is indicated by its use in OE to gloss Lat. *spelunca* and its dial. use of a 'cave, cavern, den, deep pit.'

col, OE, '*coal*, char*coal*.' Colerne (W).

cōl, OE, '*cool*.' Colwall (He), Colwell (Nb).

copp, OE, 'top, summit.' Warcop (We), Coppull, Pickup (La).

coppede, OE, 'having the *copp* or summit cut off,' hence 'pollarded,' but also 'rising to a *copp*,' hence 'peaked' and the like. We have the former in Copdock (Sf), Copthorne (Sr), Cow-beech (Sx), Copster (La), the latter in Copt Hall (Ess, Mx).

corn, OE, '*corn*,' is seldom used in OE of the growing crop, as we now employ it, and it is probable that it but seldom lies behind *Corn-* in p.n. Ritter and Ekwall have suggested that in a good many names it may be a metathesised form of OE **cron, cran*, 'crane,' a bird once very common in England. This metathesised form is made probable by the actual use in OE of *cornoc* for *cranoc*, 'crane,' and it will explain names like Cornbrook (La, Wo) and Cornwell (O) which certainly do not contain *corn* = corn. It is doubtful if this explanation can be carried as far as Ekwall would suggest, for no independent form *cron* or *corn* has been found in OE, neither is there any example of a *Corn-* name in which there are any signs of alternation between *Corn-* and *Cran-*, such as we should expect if they were really 'crane' names.

cot(e), OE, '*cot*, cottage.' The possibility of a more dignified sense is suggested by the use of OE *cotlif*, apparently as the equivalent of manor (BT *s.v.*). The pl. form is the commonest in p.n., the nom. in the numerous *Co(a)tes*, the dat. pl. in Coatham (L), Coton (C, Nth), Cotton (Nth), Cotham, Cottam (Nt). Forms which now have no sign of the pl. may well go back to OE pl. *cotu* or *cotan*. It is very often corrupted to *court* in modern times as in Maidencourt (Berks). It is very common in the compound *Calde-cot*(e), lit. 'cold cottages.' This may be simply a name descriptive of cheerless hovels or, as its frequency might suggest, may have some technical sense such as 'place of shelter from the weather for wayfarers.' It should be added that, apart from p.n. evidence, we have no knowledge of the existence of such. Froggatt (Db).

cran, OE, '*crane*.' Cranleigh (Sr). See also **corn**.

cranoc, cornoc, OE, 'crane.' Cranshaw, Cronkshaw (La).

crāwe, OE, '*crow*.' There is an OE pers. name *Crawe* (fem.) and one cannot therefore always be sure about this element, but it may be assumed in most cases. Crawley (Ha, Nb), Craycombe (Wo), Croydon (C), Croham (Sx), Cranoe (Lei).

cristelmǣl, OE, 'cross,' lit. *Christ*-sign. Kismeldon Bridge (D), Christian Malford (W).

croft, OE, '*croft*,' is used dial. of a small enclosed field or pasture, with the difference between Northern and Southern England that in the former adjacency to a house is generally understood though such is not the case in La and Ch.

croh, OE, 'saffron.' Crookham (Berks), Crowle (Wo), Croughton (Ch).

cros, late OE, '*cross*,' a Norse loan-word. Buckrose (Y).

crouche, ME, 'cross,' a French loan-word. Crouch End (Mx), Crutch (Wo).

crumb, OE, 'crooked.' Cromford (Db), Cromwell (Nt), Cronkley (Nb), Crunkley (Y). The correct pron. in all these names was once [krʌm] but a spelling one [krɔm] now usually prevails.

crundel, OE = *crundle* in the dial. of Sx and Ha. There it is said to be a 'living term' and to describe a 'ravine, a strip of covert dividing open country, always in a dip, usually with running water in the middle' (EDD). It is probably only 'living' in the sense that it is fairly common in modern place and field names and for its exact sense we must certainly take into account Grundy's statements, based upon the Charter material (*E and S*, 47–9), that it seems as a rule to be used of 'quarries or chalk-pits, especially diggings which are elongated and irregular in outline because they have had to follow the narrow lines and twists and turns of a balk or some other form of boundary.' See also Baring in EHR 24, 300. The form *crumdel*, once found, suggests that the first element in the compound is **crumb**, an etymology which would accord with the facts just recorded. Crondall (Ha), Crundel End (Wo).

cū, OE, '*cow*.' Quy (C), Quickbury (Ess), Cuffell (Ha), Cowpe (La). *cȳ* in Keyhaven (Ha), Kyo (Nb).

culfre, OE, 'pigeon, dove.' Culverden (K), Cullercoats (Nb).

cumb, OE, '*coomb*, valley,' is still in living use in SCy of a 'hollow or valley on the flank of a hill, especially one closed in at the head, on the sides of or under the chalk downs.' In OE it was of wider application. In p.n. it is specially common in D, Do, So, while it is unknown in East Anglia, Nb, Du (with one apparent exception) and very rare in Y. In Cu we have several p.n. in *Cum-* which apparently show this element but only in Cumdivock is there any evidence that the form was *cumb* rather than *cum*. As a suffix this element is very rare in La, Cu and We. See further Ekwall, *Scand. and Celts*, 109 ff. The distribution of this element at first sight favours the view that it is a Celtic loanword, but there are difficulties. The greatest is that while the element is very common indeed in D, it is rare in Co and does not seem ever to be used with a Celtic first element. Further it is not found in Breton names. As a first element it is very common in the p.n. *Compton*, to be pronounced [kʌm(p)tən] rather than [kɔm(p)tən] which is a spelling-form. Comden (K).

cweorn, OE, '*quern*, hand-mill,' in p.n. is usually compounded with **dun** and the compound denotes a hill from which millstones were quarried, the full form perhaps being *cweornstandun*, with common loss of the middle element. Quarndon (Db), Quarrendon (Bk), Quorndon (Lei), Quarrington (Du), Quarlton (La), Whernside (Y).

cyln, OE, '*kiln*.' Dat. pl. in Kilham (Nb), [kil] being a common dial. form.

dæl, OE, **dalr**, ON, 'valley, *dale*,' is still in living use in the North and North Midlands, and the counties in which it is at all common in p.n. are Nb, Cu, We, La, Y, L, Nt, Lei, Db, Nf, Sf. Isolated examples have been noted in St, Wo, So, Sx and four examples in K. In Scand. England one cannot be sure whether one has the English or Scand. word, except where the first element is a Scand. pers. name, when it is presumably the latter. Further, owing to the common use of *dale* in Northern dialect, there has been some replacement of earlier *dene*, from **denu**, by *dale* as in Oxendale (La), Arkendale (Y), Harsondale (Nb), Tursdale (Du), all of which were originally *dene*-names.

The distribution is curious. It would seem to be distinctively Anglian, and indeed North and East Anglian, except possibly for Doverdale (Wo) and the little group in K and Sx. The charter material is of interest on this point. It gives us *doferdæl* (BCS 360) for Doverdale, *imbesdæl*, with dat. *imbesdælle* (unidentified) in Ha (BCS 707) and *ruge dæl* in Ha (BCS 629), with *deopan delle* in the same charter. This points to early confusion with the allied **dell** and it may be that the Southern *dales* are really *dells*. Unluckily we have only 13th and 14th century forms for these, viz. Crundale, Dodingdale, Luckingdale, Rundal (K), Woodsdale (Sx) and Stavordale (So). These all show *dale*.

dāl, OE, 'portion or share of land, especially of a common field.' It survives in dial. *dale* and *dole* used in this sense and is more common in field-names than in p.n. Dole Hundred (W), earlier *Doleffeld*.

deill, ON, is the Scand. equivalent of **dal** and like that word is almost confined to field-names. It is very common in Y and L and in the form *dayle* was in common dial. use in ME. Howdales (L). The term seems to have been coined, or at least revived, on English soil in order to describe English agricultural conditions. See an excellent discussion of the term in Lindkvist, *P.N. Scand. Origin*, 130 ff.

(ge)delf, OE, 'digging,' hence 'quarry.' King's Delph (C), Standhill (O).

dell, dæll, OE, 'deep natural hollow or vale of no great extent.' This seems to be a distinctively Southern form and in OE charters is only found in Ha and possibly once in Berks. Dell Quay, Arundel (Sx), Fardle (D), Dell Farm (Bk). See further under **dæl**.

denn, OE, in independent use in OE to denote (i) the lair of a wild beast, (ii) a woodland pasture for swine, the two words being probably of different origin. The latter is its sense in p.n. It is found specially frequently, both as an independent word and as a suffix, in charters from the old Weald area and it was doubtless similarly used in other parts of England also. In p.n. for which we have to rely on ME evidence alone it is often impossible to determine whether we have this suffix or **denu**. The former may be suspected in forest areas. Austin (K).

denu, OE, 'valley,' used in p.n. all over England, except in those districts which have been Scandinavianised and there it is doubtless concealed behind many a present-day *dæl*. As *dene* or *dean* it is still in living use in Nb and Du, where it is applied to the narrow deep-cut valleys which are so common in those counties. As a suffix it is difficult to distinguish from **denn**; as a prefix, especially in the common name Denton it is difficult to be sure whether we have this element or *Dena* (g. pl.) from *Dene*, 'Danes,' at least in certain parts of the country. The suffix very often appears as *don* in Mod. Eng., natural confusion of unstressed suffixes being assisted by liability to topographical ambiguity, since every valley must have its corresponding hill. When this *don* follows an unvoiced consonant such as *k*, the *d* often becomes *t* and further confusion arises. Hunden (Sf), Compton (Db), Nookton (Du), Timberdine (Wo).

dēop, OE, '*deep*.' Specially common with **ford** and **denu**. Debden (Ess), Dipton (Du, Nb), Dibden (Ha), Debach, Depden (Sf), Deptford (K, W), Defford (Wo), Deopham (Nf), Dippenhall (Sr), Dibble Bridge (Y).

dēor, OE, 'animal.' Darley (Db), Dordon (Wo), Durley (Ha), Darvell (Sx), Dyrham, Deerhurst (Gl), Dereham (Nf).

dīc, OE, '*ditch, dike.*' In p.n. the term has the *ditch*-meaning of *dyke* as well as that of 'earthwork' and, except in certain obvious cases, it is very difficult to say now in what sense it is used in any particular name. Not all the Dittons are so clearly 'earthwork farms' as is Fen Ditton (C), on the line of Fleam Dyke, nor is the earthwork often so clearly visible as it is in Wrekin Dike (Du). Deighton (Y), Flendish Hundred (C), Detchant (Nb).

dierne, derne, dyrne, OE, 'secret, hidden,' used doubtless of that which one comes upon unexpectedly. Dernford (C), Darnbrook (Y), Darnhall (Ch), Durnford (St, W), Dearnley (La), Durnaford (Co), Dunford (Sr).

dor, OE, 'door, gate,' and then topographically, 'narrow pass.' Dore (Db), Mickledore, Lodore (Cu), Dorton (O).

dræg, OE, is found in several p.n. in OE charters. It is found in Drayton (Berks, Ha, Nth) in BCS 1032, 102 and KCD 736, probably in Dundry (So), *ib.* 816, in *drægstan* (BCS 699) and possibly also in Old Drax (Y) in the dat. form *Ealdedrege* (BCS 1052). It is found also in 30 or more Draytons and Draycot(t)s in the Midlands and South and in two Drayfords (D), for which we have no OE evidence. Its meaning is still a matter of discussion. It is worthy of note that the element is, in the vast majority of cases, used as the first element of a p.n. This would point to the meaning not being purely topographic in character for if it were there would be no reason, or so it would seem, why it should not be freely used as a final element. Rather it would seem to denote some material object commonly found in or about a *tun* or *cote*. Skeat advanced the suggestion that it is the common dial. *dray*, 'squirrel's nest,' but the ultimate history of that word is not known and it seems unlikely that such a word would appear in this large group of names. Ritter (*Vermischte Beiträge*, 78–80) suggests that it is OE *dræge*, 'dray' or 'drag-net,' but examination of the topography of the places in question shows that many of them are right away from water, on the slopes of downs, etc. The suggestion has also been made that we should compare ON *drag*. Ekwall (*Angl. Beibl.* 1923, 28) has suggested that Scand. *drag* and OE *dræg* might have been used to denote a place where timber is dragged or where a boat is dragged overland to cut off a river-bend. Cf. the sites of Drayton (Nf), Draycot (Db), Drayton (Berks), Drayton near Dorchester (O).

drag, ON, used in various topographical senses, but chiefly of a small hollow or glen. Dundraw (Cu), Draughton (Nth, Y).

dreng, late OE, **drengr**, ON, 'young man, lad, servant' with no special technical sense. On English soil the word came to denote a man holding by a particular form of free tenure, combining services and money payments with a certain measure of military duty. The word was already in use in OE at the end of the 10th century and long survived the Conquest. In Norse it was also used as a nickname and that may be its use in Drinkstone (Sf), Dringhoe (Y), while in Dringhouses (Y) and Drointon (St) we probably have the common noun.

drȳge, OE, '*dry.*' Driffield (Gl) and numerous Drybecks and Dryburns.

dūn, OE, '*down*, hill,' often used of a very slight slope. Farringdon (Berks), Dowland (Co). When the vowel is shortened as in Dunclent (Wo), Donhead (W), Dutton (Ch), it is not always easy to distinguish it from the pers. name *Dunn(a)*. As a suffix it is often confused with **denn** and **tun**. Quarrington (Du), Quarlton (La).

dweorg, OE, '*dwarf.*' Dwariden (Y), Dwerryhouse (La).

ēa, ēu, OE (Anglian), 'island,' must be inferred from several p.n. in Bede, e.g. *heoroteu = insula cervi* and such a form as *Lindisfarna ea* in the Mercian OE Martyrology. The more common form is **eg, ieg**.

ēa, OE, 'river, stream.' Eaton (Db), Eton (Bk). Found also in the river-name Ree, Rea (v. **æt**).

ēaland v. **ēgland**.

eald, OE, **ald**, Angl., '*old.*' In some such names as Oldland (Gl) it may have a specialised sense like the dial. *old-land* and denote land that has long remained untilled. Very difficult to distinguish from the pers. name *Eald(a)*. Aldglose, Yaldham (K).

ēamōt, OE, 'river-meet,' used of the confluence of two streams. Emmott (La), Eamont Bridge (We).

earn, OE, 'eagle,' but it is almost impossible to distinguish it from the pers. name *Earn(a)*.

ēast, OE, '*east,*' found in the numerous Astons, Eastons, Astleys, etc. The compar. form is found in Asterley (Sa). E(a)sedike (Y), Astol (Sa), Astrop (Beds).

ecg, OE, '*edge.*' Badenage (So), Hathersage, Heage (Db).

edisc, OE, 'enclosed pasture, park.' Cf. the OE glosses '*edisc, deortuun*, broel,' '*broel, hortus cervorum* deortuun *vel* edisc' (BT). The word must be identical with *eddish*, which first appears in the 15th cent. meaning 'aftermath of grass,' possibly also 'brushwood.' In the OE charters it is the equivalent of *agellus* (BCS 225). In p.n. it probably has the OE meaning rather than that which developed later. Standish from **stan** (Gl, La), Bendish (Ess) from **bean**, Thornage (Nf), Greatness (K).

efes, OE, '*eaves*, border,' especially of the edge of a wood, also of the brow of a hill. Habergham Eaves (La).

ēg, īeg, OE, **ey**, ON, 'island,' as we now understand it, and also
'land in the midst of marshes and the like.' In many cases the
evidence of the island character is not so clear now as it once was.
Eye (Sf), Sandy (Beds), Eyton (Sa), Arlesey (Beds). In East
Anglia it has undergone a corruption found also elsewhere at times.
In p.n. like Mersey, Osey (Ess), Horningsey, Whittlesey (C) where
the *ey* follows a genitival *s*, the influence of the common word *sea*
has led to a re-spelling with final *-sea* as in Mersea, Osea. This *ea*
has spread even to names in which there was no preceding *s* as in
Manea and Stonea (C). Stiffkey (Nf), Bolney (Sx), Battersea (Sr),
Hornsea (Y), Long Eaton (Db), Iford (W), Billinghay (L), Bevere
(Wo). Eyam (Db) shows the dat. pl.

ēgland, īegland, '*island*,' with the same topographical ex-
tension as for **eg**. Confused in later times with **ealand**, used of
the same kind of ground. It is very difficult now to distinguish
them. Ponteland (Nb), Elland (Y), Ealand (L) and Nayland (Sf).
v. **æt**.

eik, ON, 'oak,' freely confused with ME *ake* from **ac** in NCy p.n.
Aike (Y), Aigburth (La), Eyke (Sf), Ayscough, Ackton, Oakdale
(Y), Akehead (Cu).

einn, ON, 'one, alone.' Ainsty (Y), Aintree (La), Anthorn (Cu).

elle(r)n, OE, '*elder*-tree.' Elsted (Sx), Elstob (Du).

elm, OE, '*elm*-tree.' Elmstead (Ess). It is very difficult to
distinguish from a pers. name found in Elmington (Nth), Elmham
(Nf).

elri, ON, 'place overgrown with alders.' Ellerker (Y).

ende, OE, '*end*,' but also 'quarter or division of a town, village
or district.' Brook End (Beds), Mile End in Colchester (Ess).

ened, OE, 'duck.' Enford (W), Enborne (Berks).

eng, ON, 'pasture, grassland,' the source of NCy dial. *ing*,
'meadow-land,' more especially in marshy places, found also
occasionally elsewhere. It is much more common in field-names
than in p.n. and it has been assumed in explanation of p.n. in *-ing*
far too frequently. Ekwall (*English PN in -ing*, 28–9) shows that
it must not be assumed unless the early forms show *eng* rather than
ing. Halling (Y), Mickering (La).

eofor, OE, 'boar,' is doubtless found in a large number of p.n.
in *Ever-* but it is almost impossible to distinguish it from the pers.
name *Eofor*.

eorþ, OE, '*earth*,' found only in p.n. from *eorþburh*, used in OE
charters. Ekwall demonstrates this for Arbury (La) and suggests
it for Arbury (C, Herts), which have old camps. He notes also that
Burrow-on-the-Hill (Lei) was *Erdborough* in 1316.

ēowestre, OE, 'sheepfold.' Austerfield (Y), Ousterley (Du),
Osterley (Mx).

erg, ON. In *Orkneyingasaga* when Earl Rögnvald was trying to find Thorbjörn in Caithness, he went up a dale at night and found lodging in a certain *erg*, 'which we (i.e. the Norsemen) call **setr**, i.e. mountain-pasture.' In the same saga some 'deserted shealings' are called *Asgrimeserg*. These two passages show its primary sense and agree with the meaning of Gael. *airidh* from which the Norsemen in Ireland or Scotland borrowed the word. That is defined as 'a shealing, hill-pasture, summer residence for herdsmen and cattle, a level green among hills.' (See further Battersby's excellent note in Moorman, *PN of the West Riding*, 216–8.) The term must have gained a wider significance in England for it is often used of places which certainly were never mountain or hill-pastures. Feizor, Golcar (Y), Docker, Mansergh, Sharrow (We), Anglezark (La), Arrow (Ch). Nom. pl. in Battrix, Arras (Y), dat. pl. in Arram, Argam, Airy Holme, Eryholme (Y), Arkholme (La).

ersc, ærsc, OE, is only found in charter material but its meaning may be assumed to be the same as dial. *earsh, arrish*, used of a stubble field and also of the aftermath in SCy. Owing to its comparative rarity it has often been confused with other suffixes in p.n. Ryarsh (K), Pebmarsh (Ess), Beynhurst (Berks), Burwash (Sx), Lagness (Sx), Langrish (Ha), Irish (Co), Wonersh (Sr).

erþ, ierþ, OE, 'ploughed land, arable land.' Cornard (Sf), Bridzor (W), Brightside (Y), Hengarth (La).

eski, ON, 'place grown over with ashes.' Escowbeck (La), Eastoft in Adlingfleet (L).

eyrr, ON, 'sandbank.' Ayre (La), Ravenserod (Y) (now under the sea).

fæger, OE, **fagr**, ON, '*fair*, beautiful.' Fairley (Nb).

fælging, OE, 'fallow-land,' a derivative of **fealh**. Falling, Falinge (La).

fær, OE, 'passage, track.' Hollinfare (La), Laver, Walkfare (Ess).

fæsten, OE, 'stronghold.' Holdfast (Wo), Brinfast (Sx).

fāg, OE, 'stained, variegated.' Fawside (Du), Fawcett (We), Facit (La), Fawler (O), Foolow (Db). From the weak dat. sg. *fagan* come Fownhope (He), Faintree (Sa). Frome Vauchurch (Do), Vowchurch (He) show WCy voicing of *f* to *v* and are the English equivalents of Sc. Fa(l)kirk. It is sometimes difficult, at least in NCy, to distinguish this from **fealg**. In compounds with *church* it may refer to the colour-effect of the stonework or it may describe a half-timbered building. In most other cases it probably refers to the colour of the soil. Voaden (D).

fal(o)d, OE, '*fold*,' but not confined as it usually now is to 'sheepfold.' In OE it glosses *ovile, stabulum, bovile*. Vaulde (He), Cuffell (Ha), Darvell (Sx).

fall, ON, 'place where trees have been felled.' Threlfall (La). Ekwall cites examples of its use to denote enclosures from woodlands.

fealcen, fealca, OE, '*falcon.*' Falkbourne (Ess), gen. pl. in Fawkham (K).

fealh, fealg, OE, 'ploughed land,' later 'ploughed land left uncropped for a whole year or more,' '*fallow* land.' The nom. gives ME *falegh, fal(u)gh*, dial. *faugh* (Nb) and *fauch* (Sc), pronounced [faf], while the dat. case gives *falwe, falou* in ME and *fallow* in Mod. Eng. It is often very difficult to distinguish this element from **fealo**. Fallodon (Nb), Falthwaite (Y), Fallowfield (La), Felpham (Sx).

fealo, OE, 'pale yellow or red-coloured, like withered grass or leaves.' Without the OE forms it is very difficult to distinguish it from **fealh**.

fearn, OE, '*fern.*' Faringdon (Berks), Farleigh (Ha, K, So), Farley (Sr), Farnborough (Berks, K), Farmborough (So), Vernham's Dean (Ha), Fairley (Sa).

fearnig, '*ferny.*' Fernilee (Nb).

fearr, OE, 'bull.' Farcett (Ha), Fazeley (St).

feld, OE, Mod. Eng. *field.* These though etymologically identical differ widely in meaning. Stevenson puts the case clearly (*Phil. Soc. Trans.* 1895–8, p. 531) when he points out that OE *feld* was just the opposite of our *field*, for it meant a great stretch of unenclosed land, and the Dutch use of *veldt* brings this home to us. Arthur Young uses *field land* as a term opposed to *woodland* and we may note that in BCS 464 a grant is made to the abbey of Peterborough of land with *feld* and *wudu* and *fenn* thereto pertaining, the three apparently covering all possible types of land. This must be its sense in the great majority of p.n. in which it is found. It could only have the modern sense in those of quite recent origin. It is corrupted to *ville*, especially in the WCy, as in Glanville (D), Cheney Longville (Sa), Enville (St). Note also Cavil (Y).

fell, fiall, ON, 'mountain, hill, *fell.*' Common in NCy dial. and therefore no definite criterion of Scand. settlement. Hampsfield (La).

fenn, fænn, OE, 'dirt, mud,. *fen.*' Fenacre (D), Venn (He), Venn Ottery (D), Ratfin (W), Gorvin, Hawson (D). There are definite traces of a ME form *fann* in such names as Bulphan, Fanton (Ess), Vanne (K), Fambridge (Ess).

fennig, '*fenny*, muddy.' Sutton Veny (W).

feorðung, OE, 'fourth part.' Allfarthing (Sr).

ferja, ON, 'ferry.' *ferry* in p.n. of any age seems to be confined to the Danelaw and must be assumed to be of Scand. origin. Ferrybridge (Y), Ferriby (L, Y).

filiþe, OE, 'hay.' Filleigh (D), Feltham (So).

fīn, OE, 'heap of wood' and **fina**, 'woodpecker,' must be found in some p.n. such as Findon (Sx), but they are almost impossible to distinguish from the pers. name *Finn*.

flasshe, flosshe, ME, 'pool, marshy place, *flash, flosh*,' still used in NCy, Ch, Sa. Cf. ME *flask* used in the same sense and Damflask (Y). These must go back to Dan. *flask(e)* used in p.n. of a 'creek with shallow water, swampy or low-lying stretches of grass-land,' senses closely paralleled by the illustrations for *flash* in NED. The distribution of the term and its close semantic relation to the Danish word suggests that it is a Scand. loan-word, with common substitution of English *sh* for Scand. *sk*, assisted in this case by the better onomatopoeic effect, as of plashing through water, produced by the new English form. Flass (Du).

flat, ME, a loan-word from ON *flǫt*, denoting a level piece of ground, is specially common in field-names where it is used of one of the larger portions into which the common field was divided. Flatworth (Nb), Tarn Flat (La).

fleax, flex, OE, '*flax*.' Flaxley (Gl), Flexborough (Sx).

flēot, OE, **fljót**, ON, 'creek, inlet, estuary.' Fleet (Ha), Benfleet (Ess), Fleetham (Nb), Hunslet (Y). In Scand. England it is impossible to keep the two words apart.

flōde, OE, 'channel of water,' used as a gloss for *cloaca, lacunar*. Found in p.n. in Ha and Berks. Grundy (*E and S*, 54–5) shows that it is specially applied to intermittent springs, notably those which burst out in the chalk downs at intervals of several years. Fulflood (Ha), Inglewood (Berks).

flōr, OE, '*floor*.' Its exact sense in p.n. is uncertain. It may refer to a threshing floor or some other such floor or it may have developed something of the sense of its German cognate *flur*, the common term for a field. In Fawler (O), in which it is compounded with **fag** it may refer to a tesselated pavement. The hall of Heorot had a *fagne flor* (*Beowulf* 725).

fola, OE, '*foal*.' Foulridge (La).

folcland, OE, or *folk-land*, i.e. land descending according to folkright or common law. Faulkland (So).

ford, OE, '*ford*,' is very common in the form *forth* in p.n. forms from 1300 onwards. This is not due, as has been suggested, to association with ON *fjǫrðr*, '*firth*,' which was never loaned into English but is due to a regular phonetic development of final *rd* in an unstressed syllable. Ford (Nb), Spofforth (Y), Baxterwood (Du), Flatworth (Nb), Clanver End (Ess), Broadward (Sa), Harvington (Wo).

fors, ON, 'waterfall, *force*.' Hall Foss (Cu).

forsc, OE, pl. **froxas**, 'frog.' Froxfield (Ha, W), Frostenden (Sf).

fox, OE, '*fox*.' Foscote (W), Fewston (Y).

fox-hole, ME. Foxhall (Sf).

fugol, OE, 'bird, *fowl*.' Foulness (Ess), Foulmire (C), Fulmer (Bk). One cannot be always sure that one has not the OE pers. name *Fugol* (rare).

fūl, OE, '*foul*, dirty,' is very common in such p.n. as Fulford, Fulwell. Fulford (So) is *sordidum vadum* in BCS 476. Some of these names may contain the adj. *full* but that element is exceedingly rare in p.n. to judge by the unambiguous charter material. Foulford (Ha), Fooden (Y), Philip (Nb), Fulready (Wa).

funta, OE, 'spring,' and possibly also 'stream,' is only found in charter material. Ekwall (ES, 54, 103–8) has shown it to be a loan-word from Latin through Celtic. Havant (Ha), Bedfont (Mx), Chalfont (Bk), Fovant (W).

furlang, OE, 'an area of land a *furrow-long*.' Very common in field-names. Bamfurlong (La).

fyrhþ(e), OE, 'wood, wooded country.' In ME often contrasted with *fell* and *field* in alliterative phrases. NED *s.v.* Pirbright (Sr), Firber (La), Chapel-en-le-Frith (Db). Cf. Kent dial. *frightwood*.

fyrs, OE, '*furze*.' Furze (Co, D).

gærs, græs, OE, '*grass*.' Gresham (Nf).

gærs-tūn, 'grassy enclosure.' Cf. BCS 699 '*pratumquoque quod juxta civitatem habetur, quod Saxonice Garstone appellatur*.' Garston (Gl, Ha, Herts). Still used in Sr and Sx dial. *Not* present in Garston (La) and East Garston (Berks).

gagel, gagolle, OE, '*gale*, bog-myrtle.' Gailey (St), Gomer (Ha).

gāra, OE, 'triangular piece of land,' but used later, especially in field names, of a wedge-shaped strip of land on the side of a field which results from dividing a field whose sides are not parallel into 'lands' or 'leys.' Gore Hundred (Mx), Langar (Nt), Bredgar (K), Garland (D), Overgrass (Nb).

garðr, ON, '*garth*, enclosure.' Lingart (La), Hawsker (Y), Plungar (Lei).

gāt, OE, '*goat*.' Gatton, Gatwick (Sr), Goathurst (So), Gotham (Nt), Gay(t)hurst (Bk), Gappah (D).

gata, ON, 'road, *gate*,' still in living use in NCy. It is as a rule very difficult to distinguish this from the ordinary word *gate*, 'opening,' from OE *gatu*, pl. of **geat**. One of the least ambiguous cases is the common use of *gate* in street-names in the large Northern towns.

gealga, OE, **galgi**, ON, '*gallows*.' Galliber (We), Gawber (Y), Gallow Hundred (Nf).

gear, OE, only found in charter material, but used in the same sense as dial. *yair, yare,* 'enclosure for catching fish.' Kepier (Du). Dat. pl. in Yarm (Y).

geard, OE, 'enclosure, *yard.*' Bruisyard (Sf), Lizard (Sa).

geat, OE, '*gate,*' must refer in the majority of p.n. in which it is found to some permanent 'gate' in a fence or hedge, but as has been noted by Stevenson and Grundy it can also be used of a hollow or gap which gives the effect of a 'gate' on the sky-line. Similarly it is used of a narrow passage in *Symond's Yat* on the Wye, in the *Win(d)gates* up and down England, in Whinyates (Y) and in the well-known Winnats Pass (Db) where it describes a passage through which the wind sweeps. The nom. sg. gives dial. *yat* or *yet*. The OE pl. *gatu* becomes *gate* and then in Scand. England it is difficult to distinguish it from *gate* 'road,' from **gata.** Yate (Gl), Burnyate, Pickett (Do), Bozeat (Nth), Leziate (Nf), Ditcheat, Donyatt (So), Bagshott (W). v. **hlidgeat, hlypgeat.**

geil, ON, 'ravine, cleft.' Scalegill, Galefield (Cu), Hugill (We).

geiri, ON, cognate with **gara.** Fairly common in NCy field-names and in dial. *gair* (Nb, L, Y), used of (i) a triangular piece of land in the corner of a field, (ii) an isolated spot of tender grass. Found as a first element in Garstang (La), Gargrave, Garforth (Y), Gartree Wapentake (L), but it is difficult to distinguish it from the Norse pers. name *Geir.*

geit, ON, 'goat.' Gatesgill (Cu), Gayton (La).

gil, ON, 'ravine, *gill.*'

gnípa, ON, 'hill, peak.' Knipe (We), Knipton (Lei).

gor, OE, 'dung, dirt, filth.' Gorhuish, Gorvin (D), Gorewell (Do), Gorwell (Ess).

gorst, OE, '*gorse.*' Gorse Hill (Wo).

gorstig adj. Goscote (St).

gōs, OE, '*goose,*' is specially frequent in numerous Gosfords and Gosforths, meaning 'fords haunted by geese,' a common country sight, not 'fords used by geese.' Goswick (Nb).

græf, OE, 'pit, trench, *grave,*' but in p.n. it is almost impossible to keep this element separate from

grāf(a), '*grove,* copse,' and the allied

grǣfe, used in the same sense, which became Early Mod. Eng. *greave,* used of a thicket and of brushwood.

Seldom are the forms so unambiguous as they are in Temple Grafton and Griff (Wa), which are certainly respectively from **græf** and **græfe.**

grǣg, OE, **grá,** ON, '*grey.*' Greystead (Nb), Grayrigg (Cu).

grēat, OE, '*great.*' Grateley (Ha), Gratwich (St), Greatham (Sx). Not always easy to distinguish from **greot.**

grein, ON, 'division, branch, fork, *grain*,' used in NCy of a small valley opening from another. Haslingden Grane (La), Greenah Hall (Cu).

grēne, OE, **grœnn,** ON, '*green*,' adj. Very common with shortened vowel and also with further raising of *e* to *i* before the following nasal. Greenhead (Nb), Grendon (Wa), Grinstead (Sx), Grindlow (Db), Grandborough (Bk, Wa), Little Gringley (Nt). The substantival use of this word to denote a 'grassy spot,' still more the sense of a village 'green' are of late origin. Hollins Green (La).

grēot, OE, **grjót,** ON, 'gravel,' dial. *greet.* In Scand. England the two cannot be kept separate. Greta (Cu), Greet (Sa, Wo), Greetland (Y), Girton (C), Girtford (Beds).

gríss, ON, 'pig,' NCy *grice*, is found in a good many Grisedales and Grisebecks and the like, but cannot be kept definitely apart from the same word used as a pers. name.

grund, OE, ON, 'bottom, *ground*.' It is impossible to say which of the numerous sense-developments of this word is to be postulated for a p.n. such as Stanground (Hu). Ekwall refers its use in North La p.n. to the ON word and suggests that it has the dial. sense of 'farm, especially an outlying one.'

gryfja, ON, 'hole, pit,' NCy *griff*, 'deep narrow glen,' etc. Griff (Db, Y), Grief, Skinningrove, Mulgrave, Stonegrave (Y).

há(r), ON, 'high,' possibly, like **heah,** used to denote 'chief' also. Habrough (L).

hæcc, hec, OE, dial. *hatch, hack, heck. hatch* is used of a gate or wicket, a floodgate or sluice, a grating to catch fish at a weir, *heck* is used in the last of these senses, while *hack* has a slightly different sense-development which hardly enters into p.n. Topographical knowledge can alone settle its exact meaning in each case. In Colney Hatch (Mx) it refers to a gate of Enfield Chase, in Heckdike (L) it is clearly associated with water. Hatch (So), Heck (Y), Maidenhatch (Berks).

There is the possibility of another word **hæcce,** 'fence of rails,' entering into some of these names. Toller postulates this word on the strength of the charter material (BT *s.v.*).

(ge)hæg, OE, 'hedge' and then 'enclosure.' Bromhey (K). This is the probable source of the common ME *hay*, 'part of a forest fenced off for hunting.' It is very difficult to keep this word distinct from **heg** and **hege.** Licky (Wo), Oxney (K), Littley Ess).

hæfen, OE, **hǫfn,** ON, '*haven*, harbour.' Keyhaven (Ha), Whitehaven (Cu).

hǣme, OE, pl., is not used by itself in OE but might be added to the first element in any p.n. and then used to denote the inhabitants of that place, thus *dræghæme* (KCD 736) denotes the inhabitants of Drayton (Nth). It is actually incorporated in the p.n. Ditchampton, Sevenhampton (W), Poolhampton (Ha). It is a derivative of **ham.**

hæsel, OE, '*hazel.*' In p.n. we often have the dial. [hezl] and then in Scand. England it is very difficult to distinguish it from ON **hesli.** Heazills (D), Hasbury (Wo), Monk Hesleden (Du), Hazelwood (Sx), Helshaw (Sa), Batsaddle Lodge (Nth). Halse (D, So) preserves dial. *halse.*

hæþ, OE, '*heath,*' used in p.n. of 'wild uncultivated country.' Hatton (Sa), Hatfield (Ess), Hadley (Mx), Hedley (Nb), Haydon (K), Headley Heath (Wo), Hethel (Nf).

hafri, ON, 'oats, *haver.*' Haverthwaite, Haverigg (La), Haverbrack (We).

haga, OE, **hagi,** ON, '*haw,* hedge,' then 'enclosure' and then 'messuage.' See Grundy (*E and S* 57–8) as to possible further limitations of meaning in OE charters. It usually denotes 'enclosure' in p.n. The Scand. and the Eng. term cannot be kept apart. Haw (Gl, Lei), Haigh, Turnagh (La), Briary, Becca (Y), Wellow, Thorney, Belaugh, Bylaugh (Nf), Bilhagh (Nt), Haugh (L), Locko (Db), Little Haugh (Sf).

haining, ME, 'the preserving of grass for cattle, protected grass, any fenced field or enclosure,' still used in NCy dial. A loan-word from Dan. *hegning,* used of enclosed as opposed to common land. Haining (Du, Nb), Heyning (L), Hyning (La).

hālig, OE, '*holy,*' becomes North. ME *hāly* and South. *hōly* which, with the usual shortening of a long vowel in a trisyllable, should give Mod. Eng. *Halli-* and *Holli-* in p.n. but these have often been replaced by forms due to the independent word *holy* in St. Eng. Hallatrow (So), Halliford (Mx), Hallikeld (Y), Holystone (Nb) and numerous Halliwells, Holliwells, Holywells, and Halwills. Halstock (D).

hals, ON, 'neck,' NCy and Sc. *hause,* used for a 'connecting ridge, a *col.*' Esk Hause (Cu), Wrynose (La).

hām, OE, is used in the first instance of a farm or estate (Lat. *praedium, praediolum*) and then in the more technical sense of a vill or a manor. Thus we have *biscopham* used of an episcopal (cf. Bispham, La) and *cyneham* of a royal manor. A passage in the OE trans. of Bede suggests that it was thought of as denoting something larger than a **tun** for the Latin *inter civitates sive villas* is rendered *betwih his hamum oþþe tunum.* For *ingaham*-names v. **ing.**

Its precise significance as a p.n. element is difficult to determine. Its distribution would suggest that it was passing out of use as the English conquest advanced westwards. The counties in which

it is most frequent are Nf, Sf, Ess, C, Sr, Sx, while it is comparatively very rare in Db, Ch, Sa, He, Gl, Wa, Wo, St. There is no
evidence that it continued in use as a living suffix as late as the
Norman Conquest. At present we are hardly in a position to
translate it by other terms than those used for tun, viz. 'farm'
or 'manor.' Consideration of the distribution, meaning and use
of this term is rendered more difficult by its liability to confusion
with

hamm, OE. This confusion is already fairly common even in OE
documents themselves and it is even more likely to arise if we have
only ME forms. ME *ham* in unstressed syllables remains as *ham*
in spelling, though the vowel is shortened, while *hamm* appears
as *ham* or *hom*. Unless therefore we have an OE form preserved or
a tell-tale form in ME with double *m* or with *o*, it is very difficult
to know which suffix we have.

hamm denotes 'enclosed possession, fold,' the word being allied
to the vb. *hem*, 'shut in.' It is the source of dial. *ham*, confined to
the South and South Midlands, and denoting 'flat low-lying
pasture, land near a river,' but it is not clear whether the association with water was already developed in OE. It may have been
in such compounds as *flodhamm*, *wæterhamm* and possibly in
mylenhamm but this was certainly not always the case. Its common
use to denote land in the bend of a river may have been influenced
by the word *hamm*, 'bend of the knee.' It is very doubtful if
we are justified in finding this suffix in NCy p.n. at all.

Both *ham* and *hamm* are often confused with holmr, the former
in Barholm, Bloxholm (L), Hestholm (Y), the latter in Kingsholm
(Gl). *ham* is present in Appledram (Sx).

hāmsteall = hām + steall, OE, is used in OE as an alternative
gloss to tun for Lat. *praediolum*, used of the 'garden' of Geth-
semane. Dial. *homestall* is used of a 'farm-house and adjacent
buildings, farmyard and appurtenances, place of a mansion-house,
enclosure of ground immediately connected therewith.' It is clear
that in this compound ham has developed that further sense of
'dwelling, abode' which it had in OE, beside those given above.
Hempstalls (Ess), Hamstalls (Gl).

hāmstede = hām + stede, OE. In this compound, as in hamsteall, we must have reference to the actual site of the chief house
of the farm or manor. It is often found by itself and in compounds
in Nf, Ess, Herts, Mx, Beds, Berks, Bk, Gl, Sx, Wt, D. Sometimes
it takes the form *Hempstead* as well as the more common *Hamp-
stead*. In some p.n., such as Berstead (K), Tisted (Ha), the *ham*
element is found in the OE form of the names. Further in OE we
find some p.n. in *-ham* with alternative forms in *-hamstede* as in
the case of Sidlesham, Bracklesham (Sx) (BCS 132).

hāmtun = ham + tun, OE, though some, such as Hampton Lovet (Wo), are from **hamm** + **tun**. A good many ME *hamton* forms go back also to OE *hean-tun* (v. **heah**), to judge by such forms as *Henton*, *Hanton*, though even here the *n* is not absolutely conclusive evidence. The precise sense of *ham* + *tun* is difficult to determine. It would seem to refer to the presence of a (?) defensive **tun** around a *ham* but the compound came early to mean something very like the modern 'home farm' and denoted the centre of an estate in contrast to its outlying farms or other properties. The compound is fairly common by itself and, when in combination with another element, that seems to be some descriptive word rather than a pers. name, e.g. **broc** in Brockhampton *passim*, **ceosol** in Chiselhampton (O), **brycg** in Bridgehampton (So), **stræt** in Strettington (Sx), **norð** in Norrington (Ha). Many modern *-hamptons* do not contain this element at all.

*hamel, OE, must be assumed on the basis of the charter material and of numerous p.n. in *Hamble-* and *Humble-* in Modern English. It is an adj. related to OE *hamela*, 'mutilated person,' and MHG *hamel*, 'steep abrupt cliff,' *hamel-stat*, 'shelving terrain.' Its exact sense in English remains to be determined by careful topographic investigation. Hambledon (Ha, Do), Hambleton (R, Y), Humbledon (Du), Humbleton (Du, Nb), Hambleden (Bk), all of which really end in **dun**, and, possibly, Hamble R. (Ha).

hangra, OE, 'wood on a slope, *hanger*.' In unstressed positions it is liable to various corruptions. In the WCy where it is often found as *honger* in ME, it is specially liable to confusion with the word *hunger* and is often so spelt. Oakhanger (Ch), Clehonger (He), Clinger (Gl), Shelfanger (Nf), Songar (Wa), Binegar (So), Barnacle (Wa), Rishangles (Sf).

hār, OE, 'grey, *hoar*,' is often applied to stones and trees, especially when they are lichen-covered. OE *har-stan*, lit. grey or old stone, survives as *hoarstone* (Sc. *hairstane*), 'boundary-stone,' and is present in disguised form in Harsondale (Nb), Harsenden, Hastingley (La). *har* is very common in other compounds also, even if we take into account the possibility that in some cases we have OE *hara*, 'hare,' and it is noteworthy that in a large number of cases the places are on the bounds of a county or parish. This led Duignan to advance the view that from its use in **har-***stan* the element *har* may be descriptive of a 'boundary' in other compounds also. The examples which he adduces and observations on the site of other places seem to prove his theory.

Hoarwithy (He), Whorridge (D), Horewell (Wa), Harrock (Wo), are all certain cases of *har* rather than *hara* and in Whorridge, Horewell it is difficult to see how *har* can have any of its ordinary meanings.

hassuc, OE, 'coarse grass, *hassock*.' Haske (D), Haxmore Farm (W).

haugr, ON, 'hill, barrow, *how*,' used in ON and probably also in English of a hill whether natural or artificial. In its ME form *howe* it is very difficult in Scand. England to distinguish it from *howe* from the dat. sg. of **hoh**. Where the first element is a Scand. pers. name we may assume that we have the Norse rather than the English word. Carlinghow (Y), Ulpha (Cu, We), Gallow Hund. (Nf), Greenah Hall (Cu), Becconsall (La), dat. pl. in Holme-on-the-Wolds (Y), Hoone (Db) and possibly Haume (La).

heafoc, OE, '*hawk*,' is present in many p.n. but it is difficult to distinguish it from ON *haukr*, used as a pers. name = *Hawk(e)*.

hēafod, OE, '*head*,' and used in various senses in p.n., the chief being that of ground which by its outline suggested a head. Where it is used after an animal's name it may refer in some cases, as Bradley suggested, to a custom of setting up the head of an animal, or a representation of it, on a pole, to mark the meeting-place of a hundred. In boundary marks it is used to denote the *headland* where the plough turned after ploughing the parallel strips of the corn-land. Manshead (Beds), Swineshead (L), Fineshade (Nth), Farcett (Hu), Shepshed (Lei), Hartside (Nb), Lindeth (La), Broxted (Ess), Macknade (K).

hēah, OE, '*high*,' and possibly in some p.n. 'chief,' as in 'high street' and similar expressions. In dial. the word is variously pronounced with the vowels [ai], [ei], [i·] and these forms are found in p.n. also. Further a great many of these show forms going back to the weak dat. sg. *hean*, e.g. Henley from (*æt þæm*) *hean leage*, and these again give rise to fresh forms in *Hen-*, *Han-*, and *Hean-*. Highworth (W), Heage (Db), Heaton, Healey *passim*, Heeley (Y), Henley *passim*, Heanton (D), Henbury (Gl, W), Hinton (Ha), Hampton-in-Arden (Wa), Handley (Db), Hanbury (Wo).

heald, OE, 'sloping, inclined.' Hawstead (Sf), Halstead (Ess).

healh, OE, 'corner, angle, secret place, recess.' Such are some of the meanings of this term in ordinary OE usage. Bede equates it with Latin *sinus*, 'bay.' In BCS 225 we have in a list of boundaries '*in quoddam petrosum clivum et ex eo baldwines healh appellatur*,' suggesting association with a rocky slope, but one should probably not lay too much stress on the 'rocky.' Grundy on the evidence of the charter material says that it means a 'small hollow in a hillside or slope.' All these senses can be reconciled if we take the primary idea behind *healh* to be something 'hidden,' the word being ultimately allied to **holh**. The nom. sg. form survives in NCy *haugh*, pronounced [ha·f] in Nb and [ha·χ] in Sc., where it is used of the flat alluvial land by the side of a river, formed in its bends.

The dat. sg. gives *hale*, similarly used in dial. and also applied to a triangular corner of land. It is one of the commonest of all p.n. elements. The nom. sg. *haugh, halgh* is confined to Northern England. The form *hale* from the dat. sg. is often confused with **hyll** and **heall**. Hale (Ch), nom. pl. in Hales (St), dat. pl. in Halam (Nt). Willenhall (St), Beard Hall (Db), Stancill (Y), Lobsell (W), Northolt (Mx), Taxal (Ch), Hepple (Nb), Renhold (Beds), Roall (Y), Haulgh (La), Kirkhaugh (Nb), Earnshaw (L). *healhtun* gives Halloughton (Nt), Hallaton (Lei), Holton (O, So), Halton (Nb, Sa), Haighton (La).

heall, OE, '*hall*,' hence 'manor-house' is not common in p.n., where it seems to be of post-Conquest origin, except possibly where it is compounded with **stede** and gives such names as Halstead (La, L). Most modern p.n. in *-hall* go back to ME *hale* (v. **healh**).

hēap, OE, '*heap*,' hence 'hill.' This is suggested by Ekwall for Heap, Heapey, Hapton (La) and more doubtfully for Shap (We). Not found in OE charter material.

hearg, OE, 'sacred grove, heathen temple.' Harrow (Mx), Peper Harrow (Sr), Harrowden (Nt).

hēg, hīeg, OE, '*hay*,' is difficult to distinguish from **hege**, (ge)**hæg**. It is probably found in most of the English Haydons. Hayley (Ha).

hege, OE, 'hedge,' is very difficult to differentiate from (ge)**hæg**. Haylot (Sa).

heim, ON, 'homestead,' often interchanges with its English cognate **ham**.

helm, OE, **hjalmr**, ON, primarily 'helmet,' but used in p.n. of something which resembled or fulfilled the functions of a helmet. Thus the Norse word and dial. *helm* are used of a cattle-shed. Possibly this is its sense in p.n. Its distribution suggests Norse rather than English origin for this element. Helm (Nb, Y), Helme Park (Du), Helmshore (La).

henge, OE, 'hanging,' 'precipitous.' Hinchwick (Gl), Inchfield, Hengarth (La), Hinchcliffe (Y).

hengest, OE, 'horse, stallion.' Henceford, Henscott, Hexdown, Hiscott (D), Hingston Down (Co), but it is difficult to distinguish it from the pers. name of the same form.

henn, OE, '*hen*,' but it is difficult to distinguish this from *hean* (v. **heah**). Henley (W), Hendale (L).

hēope, OE, 'dog-rose, *hip*.' Hipbridge (L), Hepple, Hepden (Nb), Hebden Bridge (Y), Hetton-le-Hole (Du). Difficult to distinguish from a closely similar pers. name.

heordewic, OE, the source of many *Hardwicks*, is derived from *heord*, 'flock,' rather than from *hierde*, 'shepherd,' as suggested in NED. Vinogradoff (*Growth of the Manor*, 224), says that it refers to a pastoral settlement, but usually signifies the grange and stable in a small manorial settlement, as opposed to the **berewic**.

heorot, OE, 'stag, *hart*,' in names in *Hart-* (*passim*). Hurtmore (Sr).

here, OE, 'army,' especially 'raiding army.' Hereford (He), Harvington near Evesham (Wo), Harefield (Mx), Harwich (Ess).

herebeorg, OE, used once in the sense 'army-quarters.' ME *herberwe*, reinforced by ON *herbergi*, has given rise to such names as Harbour House (Du) and the numerous *Cold Harbours* throughout the country, meaning 'place of shelter from the weather for wayfarers.'

herepæþ, OE, lit. 'army-path,' used, says Grundy, of 'any through road of any age, Saxon or pre-Saxon,' but usually of the former. Harepath (D), Harpford (So), Harford, near Crediton (D).

hēse, hǣse, hȳse, OE, only found in charter material but used of 'woodland country, land with bushes and brushwood' (BT). The cognate Germ. *hees* (OHG *he(i)si*) is applied to similar country, and Low Latin *heisia* = silva sepibus septa. Hayes, Heston (Mx), Heysham (La), Tapners (K).

hestr, ON, 'horse.' Hesket (Cu), Hesketh (2La, 2Y), Hestholm (Y).

hīd, hīgid, OE, '*hide*,' denoted in the oldest times a holding which supported an ordinary free household. It came to denote a measure of land of which the size must have varied between one region and another. Common as Hyde (*passim*) and disguised in Hullasey (Gl) and Tilshead (W). Groups of five, of ten, and of other multiples of ten hides were common and have given rise to *Fyfields* and *Fiveheads* in various parts of England, to Tinhead (W) and Combe-in-Teignhead (D) and Piddle Trenthide (Do).

hielde, helde, OE, 'slope, declivity.' Tyler Hill (K), Merrils Bridge (Nt), Murrells End (Wo), Stockeld (Y).

hīgna, OE, gen. pl. of *hīwan*, 'members of a family,' and specially of a monastic community. Hinton Martell (Do), Hinstock (Sa), Henwood (Wa), Hainault (Ess).

hind, OE, '*hind*, female of the hart.' Hindlip (Wo), Heindley (Y).

hīwisc, OE, 'family, house,' and then 'measure of land on which a household is settled.' Closely allied to **hid**, the first part of the word being the same, and often used interchangeably with it in early documents. Common in S.W. England as *Huish, Hewish*. Buckish, Langage (D).

hlaða, ON, 'barn, *lathe* (NCy).' Aldoth (Cu). Nom. pl. in Laithes (Cu), dat. pl. in Lathom (La), Laytham (Y).

hlāw, hlǣw, OE, 'hill, *law, low* (dial.),' is used of a hill, especially a rounded one, either natural or artificial. Grundy says that in the charters it always denotes a tumulus and the Db *lows* are all said to be burial mounds. It is certain, however, that in NCy the term is of wider application and it may also be so elsewhere. In the South, and still more in the South-West, it is rare in p.n. *law* is specially common in Nb and Du, *low* in Db, Ch, Sa, St, He. As a suffix it is very often confused with *-ley* from **leah**. Harlow (Ess), Spellow (La), Heatherslaw, Crawley, Kirkley, Kellah (Nb), Kelloe (Du), Rudloe (W). **hlæw** gives Lew (O).

hlēo, OE, 'shelter, *lee*.' Libbery (Wo).

hlidgeat, OE, 'swing-*gate*,' especially of one set up between meadow or pasture and ploughed land, or across the highway to prevent cattle straying. Dial. *lidgitt*, Lydiate (La), Lidgett (Y), show the normal development. Lidgate (Sf), Leadgate (Du), show the same change of form as is noted under **geat**.

hlinc, OE, 'bank, rising ground, *lynch*, *link* (dial.),' used in various technical senses as of a 'ledge of ploughland in a hillside formed gradually by ploughing in such a way as to turn the clod down hill,' 'an unploughed strip serving as a boundary between fields.' NCy *link* is used of undulating sandy ground. In p.n. one should probably take it in its more general senses. Standlynch (W), Stallenge (D). Ekwall has recently pointed out that some names in *-ling*, e.g. Swarling (K), Sydling (Do), really contain this suffix. Liscombe (Bk).

hliþ, OE, **hlíð**, ON, 'slope.' Ainstable (Cu), Adgarley (La), Kelleth (We), Bowlhead (Sr), Lydd (K), Litton (Db). Gen. sg. in Litherland (La), dat. pl. in Lytham (La), Upleatham (Y).

hlōse, OE, 'pigsty, *looze* (dial.).' Loose (K, Sf), Loosebeare (D), Luzzley (La), Aldglose (K).

hlynn, OE, 'torrent, waterfall, pool.' Lowlynn, Linshields (Nb).

hlȳp(e), OE, '*leap*ing-place, place to be jumped over' and possibly also 'steep-place' generally. Lipe (W), Hindlip (Wo), Birdlip (Gl), Pophlet Park (D).

hnutu, OE, '*nut*.' Nuthurst (Wa), Notley (Ess), Nursling (Ha).

hōc, OE, '*hook*,' may be descriptive of a place at a sharp bend in a stream or it may have the sense of its Dutch and Frisian cognates, viz. 'projecting corner, point or spit of land.' Hook (Ha, Y), Liphook (Ha).

hofuð, ON, 'head.' Used in Norse p.n. of any projecting peak, of something which resembles a head in shape and also of a source. Holleth, Hawkshead in Bolton-le-Sands (La), Howden (Y), Whitehaven (Cu). Cf. *Howth* Head, near Dublin.

hogg, ON, 'cutting, right of cutting trees,' hence dial. *hagg* and *hagwood* used in much the same senses. Hagg Wood (Nb), Barns Hagwood (L).

hōh, OE, 'projecting ridge of land, promontory,' probably identical with *hoh*, 'heel,' used in p.n. of any piece of land projecting into more level ground. Sc. and NCy *heugh*, pron. [hiuχ, hjuf], is used of a 'craggy or rugged steep, glen, deep cleft in the rocks.' In p.n. it takes the forms *hough*, *heugh*, but there are alternative forms *hoo* and *hoe* from OE *hō*, as in Luton Hoo (Beds), Wivenhoe (Ess). This element, together with **tun**, gives many names such as *Ho(u)ghton*, *Ho(o)ton*, *Hutton*, and occasionally *Haughton*. Dat. sg. *hoge*, ME *howe* has given *-how* in p.n., and in Scand. England it is difficult to distinguish it from **haugr**. This suffix is specially common in Beds and Nth, fairly so in Sf, Ess, Herts, Bk, and is very common in Nb, Du. In SCy it is of much milder significance than in the North. It is subject to many corruptions as a suffix, as in Salpho, Budna (Beds), Belsay, Kyo (Nb), Wixoe (Sf), Trunnah (La). We seem to have the nom. pl. in Hose (Lei). Hoyland (Y), Holton-le-Moor (L).

holegn, OE, '*holly*-tree, *hollin*, *holm* (dial.).' Hollinfare (La), Hulne (Nb), Holne (D), Holmside (Du), Hollington (Db), Holdfast (Wo).

holh, **hol**, OE, **hol**, **holr**, ON, noun and adj., '*hole, hollow*.' Staynah, Greenhalgh (La), Hollym (Y), dat. pl. in Hulam (Du). The adj. is specially common with **burna**, **broc** and **weg** as in Holborn, Holbrook, Holloway *passim*. Holbeach (L), Holbeam (D), Hoborough (K), Howgill (Y). See also **brocchol**, **foxhole**.

holmr, **holmi**, ON, 'islet, *holm*,' but used also of any piece of ground isolated from its surroundings. Thus it was used in Iceland of a 'meadow on the shore, with ditches behind' (Cleasby-Vigfusson). In England we have the same twofold use, the former surviving in p.n. only, the latter in dial. *holm*, 'piece of low-lying ground by a river or stream.' For the form *hulme*, from ODan. *hulm*, see Ekwall, *PNLa*. Grassoms (Cu).

holt, OE, 'wood, *holt*.' Not found in NCy. Occold (Sf), Poulshott (W), Hainault (Ess).

hop, OE, 'piece of enclosed land in the midst of fens or marshes or of waste land generally.' In ME and in p.n. we have a word *hope* used of a small enclosed valley, especially 'a smaller opening branching out from the main dale, a blind valley,' which is commonly assumed to be the same word. There is little doubt that the 'valley' sense is more common in p.n. than the 'enclosure' one but the whole question needs study. It certainly bears the former sense in the p.n. in Nb and Du, where it is most frequent, and probably also in He and Sa, the other counties in which it is most common. It seems to be unknown in England South of the Thames. Cleatop (Y), Ritherope, Bacup, Cowpe (La), Philip, Snope (Nb), Gater Top (He), Alsop (Db).

hord, OE, '*hoard*, treasure.' Hordron (Y), Hardhorn (La), Hurdlow (Db), Hordle (Ha).

horh, horu, OE, 'filth,' common in *Horton*. Harpole (Nth, Sf).

horn, OE, '*horn*,' used in p.n. of something which suggests a horn. Woodhorn (Nb).

hræfn, OE, '*raven*,' appears in p.n. as *Raven-, Ram-, Ran-, Ren-, Rem-*, but it is seldom possible, at least in Scand. England, to be sure that we have not the same word used as a pers. name. Further confusion with *ramm*, 'ram,' is also possible.

hrēod, OE, '*reed*,' should give *Reed-, Red-* or *Rod-* in p.n. as in Redbridge (Ha), Rodborne (W). Forms in *Rad-* however are also common as in Radbourne (Wa), Radham (Gl). It is often difficult to distinguish from **read** and from the pers. name *Rǣda*.

hreysi, ON, 'cairn, heap of stones.' Dunmail Raise (We), Rose-acre (La).

hring, OE, ON, '*ring*,' hence 'circular.' Ringstead (Nf, Nth), Ringmer (Ess, Sx), Eakring (Nt).

hrīs, OE, **hrís**, ON, 'shrubs, brushwood.' Risbridge (K), Ruston (Nf), Riston (L), Ryston (Nf). Dat. pl. in Riseholme (L), Rysome Garth (Y), Hamble-le-Rice (Ha).

hrōc, OE, '*rook*,' is very difficult to distinguish from a similar pers. name.

hrycg, OE, **hryggr**, ON, '*ridge, rigg*.' Different dial. developments are reflected in the common *Ridge* by the side of Rudge (Gl), Rodge (Wo), Rudgwick (Sx) and Reach (K). Courage (Berks), Elmbridge (Wo).

hryding, OE, 'clearing, cleared or *rid*ded land.' Riddings (Db), Riding Mill (Nb), Woodridden (Ess). Very common in field-names.

hrȳðer, OE, 'ox, cattle.' Rotherfield (Ha, O), Ritherope (La), Rotherhithe (Sr).

hungor, OE, '*hunger*,' is fairly common, especially in field-names, to denote places with poor pasturage or crops. It is often very difficult to distinguish it from **hangra**.

hunig, OE, 'honey,' common in compounds with some word denoting water and probably referring to its pleasantness. Honey-child (K), Honeybourne (Wo), Honiley (Wa).

hunte, ME, '*hunt*' and then 'district hunted.' This development is, according to the dictionaries, quite modern, but it would seem that we must postulate its use much earlier to explain such p.n. as Chadshunt (Wa), Bonhunt, Tolleshunt (Ess), Cheshunt (Herts), Boarhunt (Ha).

huntena, OE, gen. pl. of *hunta*, 'huntsman.' Huntingford (Gl), Huntington (He, Sa).

hūs, OE, **hús**, ON, '*house*,' is rarely found in the South, as in

Stonehouse (D, Gl), Onehouse (Sf), but is common in Scand.
England, and there, as in Scandinavia, is very common in the pl.
Woodhouse *passim*, Lofthouse, Loftus (Y). Dat. pl. in Newsome,
News(h)am, Newsholme *passim*, Howsham (L, Y), Gildersome,
Loftsome, Wothersome, Ayresome (Y). Uzzicar (Cu).

hwǣte, OE, '*wheat.*' Whatcombe, Whitcombe (Do), Watcombe
(O), Waddon (So, Wo), Whaddon (W), Whiteacre (K).

hwamm, hwomm, OE, **hvammr**, ON. The OE word is glossed
angulus, the ON word is used of a 'short valley or depression
surrounded by high ground, but with an opening on one of the
sides.' One or other of these words lies behind NCy *wham*, 'marshy
hollow, hollow in a hill or mountain,' and such p.n. as Wham,
Whitwham (Nb).

hwēol, OE, '*wheel*, circle,' suggested by Ekwall for Wheelton
(La), Wheldale (Y). Welbatch (Sa).

hwetstān, OE, '*whetstone.*' Westernhope (Du), Whetstone (Lei).

hwīt, OE, '*white*, shining.' Dialectically the term *white* is sometimes applied to dry open pasture ground in opposition to woodland and black-land growing heath. At times it is difficult to
distinguish it from the pers. name *Hwita*. Wheatfield (O), Wheten-
ham (Ess).

hwyrfel, OE, **hwirfill**, ON, are cognate terms allied to OE
hweorfan, 'to turn.' *hwyrfel* is only found in p.n. material in OE
and is there applied to a **mere**, a **dic** and a **dun** and seems to mean
'circular,' or perhaps in the first case, 'eddying.' The Norse word
is used of a 'circle' and of a 'hill with rounded top.' Whorwelsdown
(W), Whorlton (Y), at the foot of the *Whorl*, a well-rounded hill,
Quarles (Nf).

hyll, OE, '*hill*,' appears in ME as *hill* and *hull* but in p.n. the
hull forms have for the most part been levelled out in favour of
St. Eng. *hill*. Monyhull (Wa), Coppull (La), Crichel (Do), Hill,
Hull (Sa), Hulton (St), Bucknell (Nth), Hordle (Ha), Shottle,
Smerril (Db), Apsell (W), Odell (Beds), Caswell (Co), Royle (La),
Beal (Nb), Shelfield (Wa), Wardle, Caughall (Ch), Hethel (Nf).
Dat. pl. in Hillam (Y).

hylr, ON, 'pool, deep place in a river.' Lickle, Troutal (La),
Dibble Bridge (Y).

hyrne, OE, 'corner.' Different dial. forms are found in Guy-
hirne (C), Hurne (Ha), Hurley (Berks, Wa), Herne (K).

hȳrness, OE, lit. *hear*ing, then 'subjection, service, jurisdiction.'
The exact extent and nature of the jurisdiction is uncertain. At
times it seems to denote 'parish.' Berkeley Harness (Gl), Lughar-
ness (He).

hyrst, OE, 'hillock, knoll, bank' and 'copse, wood,' a twofold
sense which still survives in dial. *hurst* and is found also in the

cognate *horst* of the Low Germ. dialects. Probably the original meaning was one combining the two, viz. 'wooded height.' The normal forms in Mod. Eng. are *hirst* in the North and the East Midlands, *hurst* elsewhere. Hartest (Sf), Titness (Berks), Staplers (Wt), Copster (La), Horsebridge (Sx).

hȳð, OE, 'port, haven,' and then 'landing place on a river.' ME *hithe, huthe, hethe* in different dialects, but there is always a tendency to level out in favour of the first and St. Eng. form. Rotherhithe, Lambeth, Stepney, and Chelsea on the Thames, Maidenhead (Berks), Old Heath in Colchester (Ess), Earith (Hu), Aldreth (C), Stockwith (L), Hive (Y).

ifig, OE, '*ivy*.' Ivychurch (W).

īggoð, OE, 'islet, *eyot*.' The Aits (Sr).

ikorni, ON, 'squirrel.' Icornhurst, Ickenthwaite (La), Ickornshaw (Y).

ing[1] is found in many English p.n. and in dealing with it we may first dismiss those in which it is not original. Examples of final *-ing* from ON eng, OE (hl)inc are dealt with under those elements. Medial *-ing-* often represents the gen. sg. in *-an* of an OE weak form of a pers. name, as in Abingdon (Berks) from *Abbandun*. Such are not however to be expected in NCy where the *n* of *an* was early lost. These false *ing*-types are general and widespread but often difficult to detect in the absence of conclusive OE evidence. In addition to these types, so frequent are the legitimate *ing*-names, with *ing* medial or final, that, under their influence, *ing* may be found intruding in haphazard fashion into a large number of other names, especially medially.

Final ing, so far as it goes back to OE, is found in

(i) a number of common nouns such as cieping, fælging, feorðing, hryding;

(ii) a limited number of names, often of obscure and difficult origin, in which the suffix *-ing* has been added, as a rule, though not always, to a pers. name. Lawling (Ess) is an example of a pers. name while Clavering (Ess) seems to go back to clæfre;

(iii) a large number of names in which the pl. *ingas* has been added usually to a pers. name, but sometimes to a river-name or some other element. Billing (Nth), Barling (L) are *-ingas* names from pers. names while Avening (2Gl) and Blything (Sf) are from river-names and Hertingfordbury (Herts) from *Hertford*.

---

[1] In dealing with this element one can for the most part, at least so far as one is dealing with *-ing* and *-ingham* names, do little more than summarise the conclusions of Ekwall's book on *English P.N. in -ing*, though there is serious danger that in so doing one may understate the difficulties of the problem by failing, for lack of space, to reproduce all the qualifying statements and critical discussions in his most scholarly book.

In distribution, types ii and iii are common in the East and South-East, rare in the West and South-West.

The interpretation of type ii is difficult but Ekwall argues on good grounds that at least in the case of those p.n. formed from pers. names we must interpret them as 'X's place, stream' or whatever else it may be applied to.

Type iii when formed from a pers. name must not be interpreted as a patronymic pure and simple, 'sons of X,' but 'people of X,' 'people who have to do with X,' 'family, followers, slaves of X,' the meaning probably being almost as wide and general as in those names of this type which are derived from river-names, where it must simply denote 'dwellers by.'

Beside these, we have names with medial *-inga-* and *-ing-*. *-inga*, the gen. pl. of *ingas*, is found in such compounds as *-inga*tun, *-inga*feld, *-inga*leah, *-inga*worþ, *-inga*hamm, but is most common in *-inga*ham which must denote the **ham** of X's people, or something of that kind (v. *supra*), *ham* having the sense of 'settlement, estate' or the like, and denoting a collection of dwellings rather than a single homestead. They are, like the *-ingas* names, without doubt among the oldest English names in the country. *-ingatun* is a good deal less common and the relation of these names to the *-ingaham* ones needs careful study.

These *-inga-* names are very frequent on the Continent and specially so in the coastal districts of North-East France. In England their distribution is much the same as that of the *-ing(as)* names (v. *supra*). Unless we have OE evidence it is very difficult to distinguish *-ingatun* (*-ingafeld*, *-ingaleah*, etc.) p.n. from those in *-ingtun* (*-ingfeld*, *-ingleah*). The clue to the interpretation of such forms is to be found in such a case as that of Wilmington near Lyminge, in Kent, which in an original 7th cent. charter (BCS 97) is called *wieghelmestun*, and in an early 11th cent. endorsement is called *wigelmignctun* (sic). Bradley suggested the right interpretation of this change when he argued that the farm which was once called 'W's farm' later came to be known as 'W-*ing* farm,' in which the *-ing* indicated the past association with W, in the same general way that the suffix is used in types ii and iii above.

īw, eōw, OE, '*yew*.' Uley (Gl).

ka, North. ME, 'jackdaw,' is commonly supposed to go back to ON **ká*, cf. Norw. dial. *kaa*, but it is possible that there may have been a North. OE *cā*, parallel to Mid. ME *co*, a native word. Cawood and Cavil (Y) which began with *Ca-* in the 10th cent. have an English second element. The first element is either this English word or is a late OE loan-word from the Scand. Cabourne (L), Kaber (We).

karl, ON, 'freeman, son of the common folk,' as opposed to the noble-born *jarl*, the two words standing in the same relation as OE **ceorl** and *eorl*. Except in the compounds *butse-* and *hus-carl* this word is not found in English till about 1300. It is however extraordinarily frequent in the p.n. *Carl(e)ton* found all over Scand. England and extending into neighbouring counties, such as Beds and C, which were never really Scandinavianised. This must go back to

karla-tun, ON, 'carls' farm,' though such a form is not actually found in Norse. In some cases forms such as *Carlentun, Karlintone* in DB show that *karl* must have been Anglicised and given a pseudo-English gen. pl. in *-ena*. Some may also contain the pers. n. *Karli*.

kaupa-land, ON, 'purchased land' as opposed to 'inherited land.' Coupland (Nb), Copeland (Cu, Du).

kaupmaðr, ON, 'merchant,' gen. pl. *kaupmanna*, though in p.n. it may be a pers. name, ultimately a nickname, rather than denote the actual carrying on of trade. Copmanthorpe (Y), Capernwray (La), Coppingford (Hu).

kelda, ON, 'spring, deep water-hole, smooth-flowing stream.' NCy *keld*, 'marshy place.' Keld, Hallikeld, Kirskill (Y), Ranskill (Nt), Kelleth (We).

kiarr, ON, 'copsewood, brushwood,' Norw. *kjerr*, 'pool, hollow place, marsh, low-lying ground.' The latter is the sense of dial. *car* and the sense which we may assume in p.n. generally. Byker (Nb), Carbrook (Y). Not a definite criterion of Scand. settlement.

kirkja, ON, 'church,' especially common in the numerous *Kir(k)bys*. Curthwaite (Cu).

kleif, ON, 'steep hillside.' Claife (La), Raincliff (Y).

klettr, ON, 'cliff, rock.' Dan. **klint** (in which assimilation of *n* and *t* has not taken place). The first form is found in Cleatham (L), Cleator (Cu), Cleatop (Y), Cleatlam (Du) and the second in Clints (Nb, Y). *clint* is still used in NCy to denote a 'hard rock projecting on the side of a hill or river.'

knappr, ON, cognate with OE **cnæpp** and very difficult to distinguish from it in Scand. England.

knott, ON, Late OE *cnotta*, 'knot,' used in p.n. of a 'rocky hill or summit.' Only found in the North. Hardknott (Cu).

konungr, ON, 'king.' Coniston (La), Conington (Hu), Cunswick (We), Congerstone (Lei), Coney Weston (Sf), Coney St in York (Y), Conesby (L).

kráka, ON, 'crow,' but very difficult to distinguish from the pers. name *Kraki*. Possibly in Cracoe, Cragdale (Y), Cracroft (L).

kringla, ON, 'circle.' Cringleford (Nf), Crindledyke (Cu).

krókr, ON, 'crook, bend,' is often used in Norw. p.n. to describe position in a bend of a river, but is also used of a piece of land which is hidden away or cut off from the rest. In the sense 'odd corner, nook of land' it is very common in field-names. Crookes (Y), dat. pl. in Crookham (Nb). As a common dial. word it is not a definite test of Scand. settlement.

lā, ODan., 'water along the sea, creek.' Goxhill (L, Y), Sixhill (L).

lache, leche, ME, 'slow sluggish stream, dial. *lache, letch*,' also 'muddy hole, bog.' Shocklach (Ch), Lashbrook (D, O), East Leach (Gl), Fulledge (La).

lacu, OE, 'stream, watercourse,' and still so used in the dial. of D, So, Co, Ha. Lake (W), Standlake (O), Medlock (La).

(ge)lād, OE, 'track, watercourse, dial. *lode*.' Abload (Gl), Bottisham Lode (C), Linslade (Bk), Shiplate (So).

læfer, lefer, OE, dial. *lavers, levers*, 'wild yellow iris.' Laverton (Gl), Larford (Wo), Livermere (Sf).

lǣge, OE, 'fallow, unploughed,' not found independently but inferred from OE *lǣghrycg* later *lea-rig*, and *lea-land*. Leyland (La), Layriggs (Cu).

lǣs, OE, 'pasture, meadow-land, dial. *leaze*.' Summerlease (Co), Summerley (Db), Leziate (Nf). From the dat. sg. *lǣswe* comes dial. *leasowe* and Leasowe (Ch).

(ge)lǣte, OE, 'junction of roads, etc.' Longleat (W), Haylot (Sa).

lágr, ON, '*low*.' Laskill Pastures (Y), Lodore (Cu).

lām, OE, '*loam*,' which may be found in Lomer (Ha), is almost impossible to distinguish from

lamb, OE, '*lamb*,' in Lambley (Nt), Lambeth (Sr), Lambourne (Berks). Lamberhurst (K) is from the gen. pl. *lambra*.

land, OE, **land**, ON. The OE term is used to denote 'earth, soil, landed property, estate,' 'one of the strips into which a cornfield or a pasture field that has been ploughed is divided.' In the charter material it is very rarely compounded with a pers. name. The first element describes the tenure (e.g. **folcland, bocland, sundorland**), or the state of cultivation, e.g. *irþland, wuduland*, or the crop, e.g. *linland* from **lin**. Candlet, Swillen *al.* Swilland (Sf).

lane, lanu, OE, '*lane*.' Markland (La). Dat. pl. in Laneham (Nt).

lang, OE, '*long*, tall.' Landford (W), Lamport (Nth), Launton (O), Lagness (Sx), Longner (Sa).

launde, ME, from OFr. *launde*, 'open space in woodland, glade, pasture.' Laund (Lei).

lāwerce, OE, '*lark*.' Larkfield Hund. (K), Lavertye (Sx).

lēactun, OE, 'kitchen-garden.' Leighton (Beds, Hu, La), Laughton (Sx, Y).

lēah, OE, dat. sg. **lēage. lēa** is only found in charter material in OE but there it is very common, both by itself and in compounds. In BCS 322 it is the equivalent of Lat. *campus* and in BCS 792 it is contrasted with **hamm,** the contrast apparently being that of open and enclosed land. Etymologically it is allied to Lat. *lucus,* 'grove,' and OHG *lôh,* 'low brushwood, clearing overgrown with small shrubs.' Its history would seem to be that in the first instance it denoted woodland and then a 'clearing' in such. The great forest of the Weald is called alternatively *Andredesweald* and *Andredesleage* (ASC) and the transition stage is illustrated in BCS 669 where we have a grant *cum silva campisque ad eam jacentibus, quae Earneleia dicitur.* The association with woodland is further illustrated by the high percentage of names in *-ley* to be found in counties like Ha, Wo, St, Ch, Db which were once thickly wooded, and by the numerous compounds of *leah* with tree-names found in OE charters. Other compounds such as those with **beonet, brom, fearn, hæþ, hreod, risc, þorn** point to rough and uncultivated clearings but we have the suggestion of pasturage in compounds with **hriþer, falod, hors, sceap** and of cultivation in numerous compounds with such elements as **bere, ryge, hwæte.** It is clear from these instances that the term came to be of wide application and that one would not be justified in assuming that every *ley* was really one-time forest-land. It had probably come in course of time to mean little more than 'open country,' whether heathland, pasture or cultivated. It is very common in p.n. by itself, as in *Lea, Lee, Leigh,* but still more so as a suffix, where it is sometimes confused with **hlaw** as in Barlow (Db, Du). The suffix is rare in Y and extremely so in Cu, We, L. Crowle (Wo), Marcle, Ocle (He), Ashill (Nf), dat. pl. in Leam (Db), Lyham (Nb).

leger, OE, 'lying-place, *lair,*' but only used in OE of a grave or burial-place. The association with animals is quite late. Layer (Ess).

leikr, ON, 'play, sport,' and then place for such. Ullock (2Cu).

leirr, ON, 'clay,' **leira,** 'clayey place.' Larbrick (La), Larpool (Y).

leoht, OE, 'bright, *light,*' common with tree-names. Lighthorne (Wa), Lightollers (La), Lightbirks (Nb).

leysingi, ON, 'freedman.' Lazenby (Y), Lazonby (Cu).

līc, OE, 'body.' Lickberrow (Cu), Lickpit (Ha).

līn, OE, **lín,** ON, 'flax.' Linacre, Lingart (La), Linton *passim,* Lylands (Y).

lind, OE, 'lime-tree.' Lindeth (La), Linford, Linwood (Ha), Lingwood (Ess), Limber (L).

loc(a), OE, '*lock*ed place, enclosure.' Challock (K), Parlick (La).

lœkr, ON, 'brook.' Leek (La), Leake (2Nt, L).

lopthús, ON, lit. *loft*-house, but used of a room found in or forming the second floor of a building, to which access could be had by an outside staircase (Fritzner *s.v.*). It is probably descriptive of a house whose lower part is used as stables or as a barn. Loftus (Y). Dat. pl. in Loftsome (Y).

lundr, ON, 'grove, small wood.' Lowne (Db), Lound (L, Nt), Lount (Lei), Lunt (La), Lumby (Y). As a suffix often confused with **land** as in Rockland (Nf), Birkland (Nt). Gen. sg. in Londonthorpe (L).

lyng, ON, '*ling*, heather.' Ling (Nf).

lytel, OE, '*little*.' Litchurch (Db).

mæd, OE, dat. sg. **mædwe**, whence *mead* and *meadow*, both denoting grassland. Medbourne (Lei), Metfield (Sf).

mæl, OE, 'cross, sign.' Maldon (Ess), Maulden (Beds).

(ge)mære, OE, 'boundary,' still used in dial. *meare* of a 'strip of grassland forming a boundary,' and also of a 'boundary road.' In the charters it is prefixed to various elements such as **ac, broc, cnoll, dic, hege, lacu, pol, pytt, stan, þorn, weg** to denote that these objects were on the bounds of an estate. It is very difficult to distinguish it from **mere** unless we have the OE form or the topography is decisive for the latter. Probably found in Marten (W), Mearley (La), Merbach (He).

mapel, OE, only found in *mapel-treow*, '*maple*-tree.' Maplestead (Ess), Mappleton (Y).

mapuldor, OE, 'maple-tree.' Mappowder (Do), Mapledurham (Ha, O), Malacombe (W).

mearc, OE, 'march, boundary.' Mark (So), Marcle (He), Marden (W).

melr, ON, 'sandbank, sandhill,' dial. *meal, meol*. Meols (Ch), Rathmell (Y), Ingoldmells (L).

meol(u)c, OE, '*milk*,' indicates good pasturage as in Melkridge, Milkhope (Nb) or turbidity as in Milkwell (Du).

mēos, OE, 'moss.' Meesden (Herts), Miswell (Sx), Muswell Hill (Mx), Maizley Coppice (W).

mere, OE, '*mere*, pool,' is very difficult, except on topographical grounds, to distinguish from **mære**. Often confused with **mor** as in Tedsmore (Sa), Peasmore (Berks). Martin (La), Foulmire (C).

mersc, OE, '*marsh*.' Common by itself and in the compound *Marston*. Merston (Y), Maresfield (Sx). In NCy it sometimes appears with final *sk* as in Marske (Y).

meðal, ON, 'middle.' Melton (Lei, Sf, Y), Melton Ross, Medlam (L), Middleton in Ilkley (Y).

micel, OE, **mikill**, ON, 'great, large, *mickle*,' assumes many

different forms in p.n., partly owing to dial. differences. Mickle-
field (Herts), Michelmarsh (Ha), Michel Grove (Sx), Muchelney
(So), Mistlebury (W), Middleton *sic* (He).

middel, OE, '*middle*,' as in *Middleton* and *Milton* (*passim*), so
far as the latter is not derived from **myln**. Medland (D), Mealrigg
(Cu). It is often difficult to distinguish it from ON **meðal** with
which there has been a good deal of interchange.

minte, OE, '*mint.*' Minstead (Sx), Minety (W).

mixen, OE, '*mixen*, dunghill.' Mixen (St), Mixenden (Y).

monig, OE, '*many*.' Monyash (Db), Moneyhull (Wo), Money-
laws (Nb). At times folk-etymology may have been at work as in
Moneyfarthing Hill (He) in which the first element is Welsh
mynydd, 'hill.'

mōr, OE, 'waste land, barren land.' It is our word *moor* but,
at least in the South and South Midlands, it is used in p.n. of
'swampy ground' rather than in the modern sense in which high
ground is usually implied. Found in numerous *Mor(e)tons*, *Mur-
tons*, *Morcotes*, *Murcotts*, etc. Murrells End (Wo).

mos, OE, '*moss*, peatbog.' Common in NCy. Moze (Ess),
Moseley (Wo).

(ge)mōt, OE, 'meeting-place,' especially of two streams. Emmott
(La), Eamont (We).

mūs, OE, '*mouse.*' Musbury (La).

mūþa, OE, '*mouth*, estuary.'

myln, OE, '*mill.*' Numerous *Miltons*. Milnrow (La), Mells (So),
Millow (Beds). Dat. pl. in Millom (Cu).

myncen, OE, 'nun.' Minchinhampton (Gl), Mincing Lane (Mx).

mynni, ON, 'junction of two streams,' the etymological equivalent of **(ge)myð**. Airmyn (Y), Stalmine (La).

mynster, OE, 'monastery,' used also in the 12th cent. of a
church generally. These are what we must look for in p.n. in
minster, rather than for a large church as in York *Minster*.
Misterton (Lei, Sa).

myrig, OE, 'pleasant.' Merrifield (Co), Merevale (Wa), Marden
(Sr).

mýrr, ON, '*mire*,' used of swampy moorland. Mirfield (Y),
Myerscough (La).

(ge)mȳðe, OE, a derivative of **muða**. Its primary sense is
'opening,' but it is used in p.n. of the opening of one stream into
another. The Mythe (Gl), Mitton, Myton *passim*, Mytholmroyd
(Y).

næss, OE, **nes**, ON, 'headland, cape.' Totnes (D), The Naze
(Ess), Crossens (La).

nēat, OE, 'cattle, dial. *neat.*' Neatham (Ha), Neatmarsh (Y),
Netton (W).

neoðera, OE, '*nether*, lower.' Neithrop (O).

nese, ME, 'nose,' and then applied to a 'ness' or headland. Nesbit (Nb), Neasden (Mx), Neasham (Du).

netel(e), OE, 'nettle.' Nettlebed (O).

nīwe, OE, '*new.*' The weak dat. sg. *niwan* has given rise to a large variety of forms such as *Naunton, Newnton, Neenton, Ninham, Newington*. Nobury (Wo), Nowton (Sf), Nobottle Grove (Nth), Ninfield (Sx), Nyetimber (Sx).

norð, OE, '*north.*' Norton *passim*, Nordley (Sa), Norham (Nb), Narborough (Lei).

oddr, ON, 'point, spit of land,' the Norse cognate of **ord**. Greenodd (La), Ravenserod (Y).

ōfer, OE, 'shore, bank.' Noverton, Nurton (Wo), Haselor (Wa), Oreton (St), Orton (La, We), Nether and Over Worton (O), Over (Ch), Burcher (He). Dat. pl. in Owram (Y).

ōra, OE, 'border, margin, bank.' Oare, Boxford (Berks), Ore (Sx), Wardour (W), Clare (O), Rowner (Ha). Unless we have early forms it is often difficult to distinguish it from **ofer**.

orceard, OE, '*orchard*,' but of wider application, not being restricted to an enclosure where fruit is grown. Norchard (Wo), Orcheton (D).

ord, OE, 'point, corner, spit of land.' Ord (Nb).

oter, OE, '*otter.*' Otterburn (Nb), Atterburn (Wo).

pæð, OE, '*path.*' In the Lindisfarne glosses it is given as an alternative to **dene** and from this arose Sc. and NCy *peth*, 'hollow or deep cutting in a road, steep road.' Gappa (D), Roppa (Y), Morpeth (Nb).

parke, ME, from OFr. *parc*, ultimately identical with

pearroc, OE, 'small enclosure, *paddock*,' the diminutive of a lost OE *pearr*, dial. *par*, 'enclosure for beasts.' Parr (La), Paddock (K), Parrock (Sx).

penn, OE, 'enclosure, *pen*.' Penn (Bk).

pīc, OE, 'sharp pointed instrument,' not found in the charter material in a topographic sense. ME *pike*, 'pointed hill,' is confined to NCy and has probably been reinforced by Norw. *pik*, 'pointed mountain.' Pickup (La), Pigdon (Nb).

pigh(t)el, ME, 'small field, enclosure.' Found chiefly in field-names. Colepike Hall (Du), Pickledean (W).

pīpe, OE, '*pipe*, channel of a small stream.' Dial. 'small ravine, dingle.' Pipe (St).

pirige, pyrige, OE, '*pear*-tree.' Perry (Wo), Puriton (So), Purton (W), Potterspury (Nth), Buttsbury (Ess), Perham (W), Pirbright, Pyrford (Sr).

pise, OE, '*pease.*' Peasfurlong (La), Peasemore (Berks), Pested (Herts).

plæsc, OE, 'shallow pool, dial. *plash*,' only found in charter material. Plaish (Sa, So), Plesh (Do).

plega, OE, '*play*,' but used in p.n. to denote the place where animals disport themselves. Deerplay (La), Oterplay (K).

plegstōw, OE, '*play*-place,' glossed by *amphitheatrum, palaestra, gymnasium*, referring in p.n. to the place where village sports and the like were held. Plaistow (Db, D, Ess, Sx), Plestins (Wa).

plūme, OE, '*plum, plum*-tree.' Plumpton *passim*. Plungar (Lei).

pōl, OE, '*pool*, deep place in a river, tidal stream.' Poole *passim*, Polstead (Sf), Lappal (Wo), Cople (Beds), Poulton *passim*. Dat. pl. in Poolham (L).

port, OE, 'town,' used specially of one possessing market-rights and rights of minting, possibly also with some reference to its having defensive works, if we may judge by its frequent use as an alternative gloss to **burg** and to render the Lat. *castellum*. The numerous *Newports* were probably first so called when they were given market-rights.

prēost, OE, 'priest.' Found in numerous *Prestons, Prescot(t)s, Prestwicks*, where the first element is usually the OE gen. pl. *preosta*. It is difficult to determine whether these places were owned by priests, used for their endowment, or occupied by them. Purston (Y), Prustacott (Co), Prenton (Ch).

pūca, OE, 'goblin, *puck*, dial. *pook*.' Poughill, Pophlet Park (D), Pownall (Ch).

pull, OE, used with the same sense as **pol** and often difficult to distinguish from it. Pull Court (Wo), Overpool (Ch).

pyll, OE, 'tidal creek on the coast, pool in a creek at the confluence of a tributary stream, dial. *pill*,' still used in Co and He, a Celtic loan-word. Huntspill, Pylle (So).

pytt, OE, ME *pitte, putte, pette*, '*pit*, grave.' Only St. Eng. *pit*, as in Woolpit (Sf) and *pet*, as in Pett (K, Sx) seem to have survived.

rā, OE, '*roe*-buck.' Rogate (Sx), Rocombe (D), Raydale (Y).

rá, ON, 'landmark.' More than one *Raby* and Roby (La).

rǣge, OE, 'wild she-goat.' Rayleigh (Ess).

ramm, OE, '*ram*.' Ramshorn Down (D). Very difficult to separate from **hræfn**.

rand, OE, 'border, edge, dial. *rand, rond*.' The dial. word is used in Eastern England of a strip or border of ground in various technical senses. Only noted in ECy p.n. Rand (L), Raunds (Nth).

rauðr, ON, 'red,' cognate with **read**. Rawcliffe (2La, 3Y),

Roecliffe, Roppa (Y), Rockliffe (Cu), Rothay (We), Rathmell (Y). Not always easily distinguished from the pers. name *Rauði* or *Routh*.

rāw, rǣw, OE, '*row*.' The first form gives St. Eng. *row* and NCy *raw*, the latter dial. *rue*, 'row,' in various senses. Milnrow (La), Rattenraw (Nb), and probably Rew (Wt), Rewe (D).

rēad, OE, '*red*.' Radwell (Beds), Radford (D), Ratcliffe (Mx). Not always easy to distinguish from **hreod**.

. **refr**, ON, 'fox.' Reagill (We).

ridde, ME, 'cleared, p.p. of *rid*, to clear,' commonly derived from ON *hryðja*, but as there was an OE noun *hryding* we are probably right in assuming a corresponding OE verb which would better explain this widespread element than if we assume it to be a Scand. loan-word. Ridley (specially in Nb, Du), Redland (Gl), Rudloe (W).

riþ, riþig, OE, 'small stream, brooklet, dial. *rithe* (Sr, Sx, Wt).' The expanded form is found in Fulready (Wa), Cropredy (O) and seems to be confined to the South Midlands; the shorter one belongs to the South generally as in Hendred, Childrey (Berks), Meldreth (C), Shottery (Wa).

rod, OE, 'clearing, assart,' only found in charter material. Roade (Nth), Road (So), Odd Rode (Ch), Royd (Y). Nom. pl. in Rhodes *al.* Royds (Y). See more fully *PN Nb and Du*, 167–8. *royd* is the common dial. development in La, Y.

rūh, OE, '*rough*.' This adj. takes various forms in p.n., some going back to the nom., others to dat. case forms, especially the weak dat. sg. *rugan*, ME *rowe(n)*. Rowley *passim*, Rufford (Nt), Rusper, Roffey (Sx), Rowner (Ha), Roall (Y).

rūm, OE, '*roomy*, spacious.' Romford (Ess), Romiley (Ch), Rumworth (La), Roomwood (Nt).

rúm, ON, 'forest-clearing.' Dendron, Dertren (La). See further *PN La*, 16.

ryge, OE, '*rye*.' Found often in *Ryton, Ryley, Ryhill* and the like. Reydon (Sf), Royton (La), Ryle (Nb), Roydon (Nf).

rygen, adj. from **ryge**. Renacres (La).

rysc, OE, '*rush*.' ME *risshe, resshe, russhe* and 16th cent. *rossh, roche*. Hence many places in Rush-, Rish-. Roseden (Nb), Ruislip (Mx). Dat. pl. in Rusholme (La).

(ge)ryðre, OE, 'clearing,' allied to **hryding**, only found in p.n. Ryther (Y).

sæppe, OE, 'spruce-fir.' Sapley (Hu), Sabden (La).

sǣte, OE, 'house, *seat*,' is rare but is found in charter material. It may be confused with

sǣte, pl. 'dwellers, inhabitants' is common. It is found in names of districts such as Somerset and can be added to the first element

of any p.n. to denote the inhabitants of that place, e.g. *Ombersete*
(BCS 361) for the inhabitants of Ombersley (Wo).

Both alike appear in later English as *-set(t)* and in each case
careful consideration is needed as to which is the most likely
source. The suffix, from whichever source it may come, is specially
common in Nf, Sf. In Nb, Du it often appears as *side*. Simon-
side (Nb).

sǣtr, ON, 'summer-pasture farm, shieling.' See more fully
PN La, 16–7. It is almost always corrupted to *-side* or *-shead* in
present-day forms, as in Ambleside (We), Cadishead (La). Blen-
nerhasset (Cu), Satterthwaite (La). Very difficult sometimes to
distinguish from **sǣte**.

sand, OE, '*sand*.' Sambourne (Wa), Saunton, Sampford (D),
Sound (Ch).

saurr, ON, 'mud, dirt,' is common in the p.n. *Sowerby*. Lindkvist aptly quotes from *Landnamabók* where Steinulfr built a farm
on his new settlement in Iceland and called it *Saurbœ*, i.e. Sowerby,
'because the ground there was very swampy' (*PN Scand. Origin*,
162). Still surviving as dial. *saur*.

sceaga, OE, 'small wood, copse, thicket, *shaw*.' Dial. *shaw* is
used of (i) a shady wood in a valley (Y), (ii) a broad belt of underwood around a field. It is significant that the only compound with
a tree in OE charters is with **alor** (BCS 1331) and no compounds
with *oak*, *ash*, and *elm* have been noted. In BCS 227 we have
mention of *mariscem, vocabulo scaga*. This hardly means that *scaga*
is to be interpreted 'marsh' but points to the fact that it could be
aptly used of the low underwood which one gets on marshy ground.
Wilshers (La), Shaugh Prior (D).

sceald, OE, 'shallow,' only known in charter material. Shad-
well (Sf), Shalfleet (Wt), Shadforth (Nb).

scēap, scīp, OE, '*sheep*.' Sheffield (Sx), Shapwick (D), Shibden
(Y), Shifford (O), Shiplate (So), Shopwyke (Sx).

sceard, OE, 'notch, gap, dial. *shard*,' still used of a gap in a
hedge or bank. Shardlow (Db), Sharperton (Nb). Cognate with
skarð.

scearn, OE, 'dung, filth, dial. *sharn*.' Sharnbrook (Beds),
Sherrington (W), Sharrington (Nf), Sherwoods (Ess), Shernden
(K). For *-ing* forms cf. **cweorn**.

scearp, OE, '*sharp*, pointed, precipitous.' Sharpness (Gl),
Sharpway (Wo).

scēat, OE, 'nook, corner, point.' Bagshot (Sr), Bramshott (Ha).
It is very common in field-names.

***scelde**, ME, 'shallow,' allied to **sceald**. Shelford (Nt), Shilford
(Nb).

sceolh, OE, 'oblique, awry.' Showley (La).

4–2

schele, ME, the English cognate of ON **skáli,** used first of a shepherd's summer-hut and then of a small house, cottage or hovel. Confined to Nb, Du and South Sc. *shealing* is a derivative form. Shiels *passim*, North and South Shields (Nb, Du).

scīd, OE, '*shide*, shingle, piece of thin wood.' Shidfield (Ha).

scīene, OE, 'beautiful.' Sheinton (Sa), Shenington (O), Shelland (Sf), Shenfield (Ess). Cf. *scenfeld* used in OE of the Elysian fields and of the vale of Tempe. (BT *s.v.*)

scipen, OE, = '*shippen*, cattle-shed.' Shippen (Y), Shippon (Berks).

scīr, OE, 'jurisdiction, district, *shire*.' Its exact significance depends upon the history of the place. Found as a prefix in Shiremoor (Nb) to denote 'moor in Tynemouth*shire*' and in Shireoaks (Nt, Y) to denote oaks on the border of two shires.

scīr, adj. 'clear, shining,' as in the numerous p.n. (spelt either *Shir-* or *Sher-*) like Shirb(o)urn(e), Shirford, Shirbrook, also in Shurnock (Wo). In some cases we may have the noun **scir** used adjectivally to describe something which is on a boundary. Sheerness (K). Scandinavianised in Skyrack (Y).

scīr-gerēfa, OE, 'sheriff.' Shrewton (W).

scucca, OE, 'demon, goblin, dial. *shuck*.' Schuckton (Db), Shugborough (St), Shecklow (Bk).

scylf, OE, 'rock, pinnacle, crag,' to judge from the glosses in which it is found, but there can be little doubt that it had already developed the meaning 'shelving terrain, *shelf*' at an early date, possibly through association with the very rare and rather doubtful *scilfe* = shelf, ledge. Such must be its sense in a good deal of charter material. Shelf (Y), Shelfield (Wa), Shelley (Sf, Sx), Gomshall (Sr), Shareshill (St), Shilton (Wa), Shell (Wo), Oxhill (Wa), Minshull (Ch), Sufton (He), Bashall Down (Y).

scyttels, OE, 'bar, bolt, dial. *shuttle*.' Still used of 'the horizontal bar of a gate, a flood-gate.' Shuttleworth (3La).

sealh, salig, OE, 'willow, dial. *salley*.' The large variety of forms taken by this element in p.n. is due in part to different development of nom. *sealh* which gives dial. *saugh* (NCy) and dat. *seal(h)e* but also to the second form *salig* found in OE. Saul (Gl), Sale Green (Wo), Sawley (Y), Salford (La), Salpho (Beds), Salehurst (Sx), Saighton, Saughall (Ch).

sealt, OE, '*salt*.' Salcombe (D), Salford (O, Wa). A *salt*-ford must have been a ford on one of the old *salt*-roads.

sēað, OE, 'pit.' Roxeth (Mx).

secg, OE, '*sedge*,' is very difficult to distinguish from *Secg*, a pers. name.

sef, ON, 'sedge, dial. *seave* (NCy).' Sefton (La).

sele, OE, 'hall, building.' Newsells (Herts), Seal (K), Zeals (W).

selja, ON, 'willow,' cognate with **sealh.** Selker, Sillyrea, Silecroft (Cu).

setberg, ON, 'seat-hill,' i.e. one with a flat top. Sedbergh (Y), Sadberge (Du).

shingle, ME, has two meanings, (i) 'thin piece of wood used as a house-tile,' (ii) 'small pebbles.' The etymology of these words is obscure and in both cases we get forms with initial *s* as well as *sh*. It is the former which we usually get in p.n. We probably have (i) in Singleton (La), and (ii) in Chingford (Ess), Singlewell (K), Singleborough (Bk). See *PN La* 154.

sīc, OE, **sík**, ON, dial. *sitch, sike*, 'small stream in marshy ground, gully, stretch of meadow.' Gorsuch (La).

sīd, OE, 'broad, wide.' Sidebeet, Siddal (La), Sidestrand (Nf), Sydling (Do).

sīde, OE, '*side*,' is used in p.n. of the 'slope of a hill or bank, especially one extending for a considerable distance,' possibly also of the bank or shore of a stream. Confined to NCy. Langsett (Y), Fawcett (We).

skáli, ON, cognate with **schele** and used in the same sense. Very common in the pl. See more fully *PN Scand. Origin* 190. Seascale, Gatesgill, Horsegills (Cu), Scholes (La, Y), Scarrow (Cu), Scowcroft (La), Laskill Pastures (Y).

skarð, ON, 'notch, cleft, mountain-pass.' Gatesgarth (Cu), Scarcliff (Db). It is often difficult to distinguish it from the pers. name *Skarði*, really a nickname meaning 'harelip.'

skeið, ON. Found in Norse p.n. in more than one sense but all going back to the primary idea of 'separation,' the word being allied to *shed* in water*shed*. Its exact sense in English p.n. needs investigation. Wickham Skeith (Sf), Brunstock (Cu). In Hesket (Cu), Hesketh (2La, 2Y) it is compounded with **hestr** and denotes 'track marked off for or suitable for horse-racing.'

skírr, ON, 'pure, clear, bright.' Skirwith (Y).

skógr, ON, 'wood,' cognate with **sceaga.** Briscoe, Busco (Y), Skewkirk, Ayscough (Y), Myerscough (La). Gen. sg. *skógar* in Scorbrough (Y).

slá(h), OE, '*sloe*.' Sloley (Nf, Wa), Slaugham (Sx), Slaithwaite (Y).

slæd, OE, 'low flat valley.' Dial. *slade* is used of a 'breadth of green sward in ploughed land (NCy), a dried watercourse (Ess), a strip of greensward between woods (Nth), low flat marshy ground.' See more fully EDD. Castlett, The Slad (Gl), Bagslate (La), Weetslade (Nb).

slæp, OE, 'slippery place, dial. *slape*.' Slepe (Hu), Slape (Do, Sa), Sleap (Sa), Hanslope, Slapton (Bk).

slāhtrēo, OE, '*sloe-tree*.' Slaughter (Gl), Slaughters (Sx), but probably not in Slaughterford (Gl).

slakki, ON, dial. *slack*, 'shallow valley, depression in a hill-side or between two hills.' Distinctively West Scandinavian.

slétta, ON, 'plain, level field, dial. *sleet* (NCy).' Slates (L), Sleights (Y), Misslet (We).

*slinu, OE, 'gentle slope,' postulated by Ekwall to explain Slyne (La), Slinfold, Slindon (St, Sx). See *PN La* 185.

smæl, OE, '*small*, narrow.'

smár, ON, 'small.' Smeathwaite (Cu).

smeoru, OE, **smjǫr**, ON, 'fat, grease.' The Norse word was certainly used as a first element in p.n. to describe rich pasturage and the English word was probably similarly so used. Smerden (Wt), Smardale (We), Smerril (Db).

smēðe, OE, 'smooth.' Smedmore (Do), Smeeton (Lei), Smeaton (Y), Smithfield (L, Mx), Smithdown (La). Weak dat. sg. in Smithencote (D).

snād, snæd, OE, only found in charter material, denotes something which is 'cut off,' e.g. an isolated wood or a clearing in a wood. From *snad* we have Snodhurst (K), Snodhill (He), Whipsnade (Beds), Kingsnorth, Oxenheath (K). From *snæd* come Snead (Wo), Sneyd, Pensnett (St), Snedham (Gl).

sneið, ON, cognate with **snad** and with similar meaning. Snaith (Y).

sōcn, OE, 'right of jurisdiction,' and then the area over which it is exercised. Soke (Ha), Soke of Peterborough (Nth), Walsoken (Nf).

sol, OE, 'muddy or miry pool, dial. *sole* (K).' Barnsole, Runsell (K), Rodsell (Sr).

spær, OE, found only in charter material and then in association with forest areas. It is allied to ME *sparre*, 'balk, pole,' and probably denotes some form of enclosure. Rusper (Sx), Holtspur (Bk), Sparham, Sporle (Nf).

spánn, ON, 'chip, shaving, shingle for tiling.' Spaunton (Y).

speld, OE, 'chip, splinter of wood,' found in forest areas. Speldhurst, Spilsill (K).

spell, OE, 'speech, story, *spell*,' used probably in p.n. to describe some old place of public assembly. Spelthorne Hund. (Mx), Spellow (La).

spōn, OE, 'chip, shaving,' used also of a 'shingle.' In Spoonley (Sa) it probably refers, as in *sponleoge* (BCS 343), to a forest area. Spondon (Db).

spring, spryng, OE, '*spring*.' Some names must show the dial. *spring* = copse. Hazelspring (O), Oxspring (Y), Ospringe (K).

stæf, OE, 'rod, *staff*,' is not found in the charter material but it is difficult not to think that we have it in Staveley (Db, La), Stalybridge (Ch), which perhaps come from *stæfa-leah*, i.e. *ley* of the staves, or *ley* marked out by such.

*stæfer, OE, 'stake, pillar,' or the like, is postulated by Ritter (*Vermischte Beiträge* 125–6) to explain Staverton (Gl, Sf, W), Starton (Wa), Stears (Gl), all with ME *stavre*. He takes it to be the English cognate of Dan. *staver*, 'stake,' and quotes several continental parallels. The names thus formed are parallel to those in **stapol**. Starbottom (Y) may contain the Dan. word itself.

stæþ, OE, 'bank, shore, landing-place.' Stafford (St). In Scand. England it is very difficult to distinguish from ON stǫþ.

stān, OE, '*stone*, rock,' may have various meanings in p.n. It may denote the presence of a rock as in Dunstanborough (Nb), of some quarry, as in Whetstone (Lei), or of boundary stones, as in Fourstones (Nb), or that something is made of stone, as in Stanbridge (Beds) and probably in the great majority of the very numerous *Stantons* and *Stauntons*. Staine (C), Staines (Mx), Stondon (Ess), Stoford, Stowell (So), Stowford (D, W), Staward (Nb), Standlynch (W), Stallenge (D), Standlake (O), Steane (Nth). There has been much confusion between p.n. in *stan* and those in **tun** preceded by the gen. sg. in *-es* of a pers. name or common noun, for both alike in Mod. Eng. naturally end in *ston*. Kingstone (He) is really 'King's *tun*,' while Wroxton (O) is 'Wrocc's *stan*.' Blaxton (Y).

stapol, OE, 'post, pillar, *staple*.' Stapleton (D), Staplers (Wt), Stalbridge (Do), Dunstable (Beds), Stapleford *passim*. Sometimes confused with **stiepel** in later documents.

staðr, ON, pl. **staðir**, is the cognate of OE **stede** and in the sg. is used to denote 'site, position,' and is not compounded with a pers. name. In the pl. it is very common and there is frequently compounded with such. Frequent confusion with **stede** has occurred and it is also very difficult to distinguish it from stǫþ. Birstwith (Y), Bickerstaffe (La).

steall, OE, 'position, site, place, cattle-*stall*.' Possibly in Stalisfield (K). See further **hamsteall, tunsteall**.

stede, styde, OE, 'place, position, site.' It is only very rarely indeed that this element is compounded with a pers. name. The usual types of compound are those in which we have (i) a descriptive adj. as in Greenstead, Fairstead (Ess), reference (ii) to its trees as in Alderstead (Sr), Buxted (Sx) from **boc**, (iii) to the character of the land, as in Felstead (Ess) from **feld**, Medstead and Morestead (Ha) from **mæd** and **mor**, Densted (K), Fenstead (Sf), (iv) to its crops, as in Pested (Herts), Banstead (Sr) from **bean**, Plumste(a)d (Nf, K, Sx), Whetsted (K), (v) to some premises upon it as in Worstead (Nf) from **worþ**, Tunsted (Nf), Kirkstead (L),

Burstead (Ess), Halstead *passim*, Cowsted (K) from **cot** and **hamstede**, (vi) to animals kept there as in Swinstead (L), Horsted (Sx), Oxted (Sr), or (vii) to its use for some specific purpose, as in Chipsted (Sr) and Flamstead (Herts) respectively from **ceap** and *fleam*, 'flight,' hence 'place of refuge.' The counties in which this suffix is chiefly found are Ess, Herts, Sf, Nf, K, Sr, Sx, Ha, Wt. It is very rare in NCy except in a few names of comparatively modern origin, in which it may have the sense 'property, estate' (NED *stead*, sb. 7) and is almost equally rare in the West and South-West. The Stude (Wa), Stidd (La).

steinn, ON, 'stone, rock,' cognate with OE **stan**. It is very common in p.n. in numerous *Staintons* and *Stainforths* but is not always easily distinguished from the pers. name *Steinn*. It is often replaced in the present-day form by English *stan* or *stone*. Stenwith (L), Stanwix (Cu), Stonegrave (Y).

steort, OE, 'tail,' hence applied to a piece of land which by its shape or situation suggests such. Stert (W), Steart (Co), Gastard (W), Start Pt. (D).

sticol, OE, 'steep, dial. *stickle*.' Sticklepath (D), Stickledon (Mx) *lost*.

stīepel, OE, 'steeple.' Steeple Bumpstead (Ess). In p.n. such as Steepleton (Do) and Stapleton (He) reference must be made to a neighbouring church steeple or other such high tower.

stīg, OE, **stíg**, ON, 'path.' Ansty (v. **anstig**), Stifford (Ess), Styford (Nb), Bransty (Cu).

stīgel, OE, '*stile*,' of whatever shape or form. Henstill (D), Steel (Sa), Steelhill (Co). Dial. *steel* is still used.

stigu, OE, '*sty*.' Housty, Houxty (Nb).

stirc, **styric**, OE, 'young bullock, heifer, *stirk*.' Stirchley (Sa), Strickland (We), Storthwaite (Y).

stoc, OE, 'place,' is very rare in OE apart from p.n. material. It is found once as an alternative to **stow**. It is used in the compounds *stoclif*, *stocweard*, *stocwic*, the first two of which are glossed as *oppidum* and *oppidanus* respectively, and the third of which is used to describe the monastery on Monte Cassino. In later times it appears as *Stoke* passim, which must be from the dat. sg. *stoce*, and as *stock*, e.g. Culmstock (D). It is not always easy to distinguish it from

stocc, OE, 'stump, trunk, *stock*.' Stockland (Do), Stockleigh (D), numerous Stocktons as well as Staughton (Beds), Stoughton (Lei, Sr, Sx) in which we probably have reference to a **tun** actually made of 'stocks.'

stoccen, OE, adj., 'made of *stocks*, logs or trunks.' Middendorff quotes BCS 458, where we have reference to *lignea capella...quae anglice Stocckin appellata* (est) side by side with *lapidea capella...*

anglice stonin appellata. Stokenchurch (Bk), Stocking Pelham (Herts).

stocking, ME, 'clearing of *stocks*,' and later 'piece cleared of *stocks*.' Ekwall (*PN in -ing* 26) finds this in Stocking (St) and in many field-names.

stōd, OE, '*stud*, herd of horses.' Studley (Y), Stodmarsh (K), Stoodleigh (D).

stōdfald, OE, '*stud*-enclosure.' Stuffle (Co). It is often difficult to distinguish this from compounds with **stott**.

stofn, OE, ON, 'stump of a tree, dial. *stoven*.' Stoven (Sf), Stewnor (La).

stǫng, ON, 'pole, stake, dial. *stang*.' Stanger (Cu), Mallerstang (We).

storð, ON, 'brushwood, young plantation.' Storrs (La), Storiths (Y).

stǫþ, ON, 'landing-place,' cognate with **stæþ**, from which it is often difficult to distinguish it, as also from ON **staðr**, pl. *staþir*. Toxteth (La). Pl. in Burton and Flixborough Stather (L).

stott, OE, 'horse, bullock.' Stotfold (Beds), Statfold (D, St), Staddon (D).

stōw, OE, denotes primarily a place or site and forms in OE a series of compounds with **cot, ceap, plega, wic** and other common nouns which have left their trace in such p.n. as Costow (W), Chepstow (Mon), Plaistow (Ess), Wistow (Y). The main source however of names in *stow* in English is the use of this word to denote land dedicated to some saint or used for some religious purpose. That is its meaning in the large majority of p.n. which contain this element, whether standing by itself or used as a suffix. The first element is usually a saint's name as in Instow (D), from *Johannestou*, Wistow (Lei) from St Wigstan, while Stow-on-the-Wold (Gl) was once Stow St Edward. The parish church is as a rule dedicated to the saint in question. Sometimes we have other compounds, such as Godstow (O) and Halstow (D), from **halig**. It is the equivalent of Welsh *llan*, Bridstow (He) being known as *Lann san Bregit*. Bristol (So).

stræt, OE, a loan-word from Latin *via strata* and primarily applied to roads of Roman construction but in course of time applied by our forefathers to any made-up road. Names like Street, Stretton, Stratton, Stratford, Stretford, Stre(a)tley, Streetley, Streatham, almost without exception contain this element. Stradbrooke (Sf), Sturton (Nb, Nt), Stirton (Y), Strelley (Nt), Strete (D), Startforth (Y), Strat(h)fieldsaye (Ha), Strettington (Sx).

strand, OE, 'shore, bank, *strand*.' Overstrand (Nf), Stranton (Du).

strōd, strōð, OE, 'marshy land overgrown with brushwood,' only known from charter material. Strode (Do), Stroud (Gl), Strood (K), Bulstrode (Bk), Langstrothdale (Y), Strudwick (Nth).

strother, ME, 'marsh,' a derivative of **strod** and confined to NCy. Strother, Broadstruthers (Nb).

stubb, OE, 'stump of a tree, *stub*.' Elstub (W). Common in the pl. Nom. in Stubbs House (Du), dat. pl. in Stubham (Y).

*styfic, OE, 'stump,' is made probable by the OE vb. *styfician*, 'to root up,' and *styficung*, 'clearing.' Stukeley (Hu), Stewkley (Bk), Stiffkey (Nf).

sundorland, OE, lit. *sunder*-land, land set apart for some particular purpose. In the OE Bede it is used to translate *territorium* in reference to the lands of the monastery of Wearmouth and Jarrow.

sūð, OE, '*south*,' as in numerous Suttons, Sudburys and the like. Songar (Wa), Sowdley (Sa), Sidnal (He), Suffield (Y). Comparative *suðerra* in So(u)therton (Sf).

swān, OE, 'herd,' more especially 'swine-herd.' Swanage (Do), Swannacott (Co), Swanton (Nf), Santon (Beds). Only found in SCy p.n.

swēora, OE, 'neck, col.' Swyre Head (Do), Sourton (D).

swīn, OE, 'pig, boar, *swine*.' Swinford *passim*, Sunbrick (La), Swingfield (K), Swilland (Sf).

syle, OE, 'miry place,' derivative of **sol**. Selham (Sx), Sulhampstead (Berks), Sulgrave (Nth).

taile, ME, '*tail*,' used in Sc. of a slip of land irregularly bounded, jutting out from a larger piece, and so found in NCy p.n. Bartle (La), Croxdale (Du).

*tang, twang, OE, alike meaning primarily 'tongs' and then 'tongue of land' at the tong-like junction of two streams are postulated for p.n. by Ekwall (*PN La* 18), to explain the early forms of Tong (K, Sa), Tonge (Lei, Y), Tangley, Tongham (Sr).

tēag, OE, only found in charter material but there used as the equivalent of Latin *clausula*. As *tigh* or *tye* it is in dial. use in Sf, Ess, K, and in p.n. it is found in Teigh (R), Minety (W), Marks Tey, Tilty (Ess), Bramblety, Lavertye (Sx).

þel, OE, 'plank.' Thele (Herts), Theale (Berks, So), Thelwall (Ch).

þelbrycg, 'plank or wooden bridge.' Thelbridge (D), Elbridge (Co, K, Sx), Elmbridge (Gl).

þēod, OE, 'nation, people,' hence OE *þeodweg*, 'highway,' corrupted to the Ede Way (Bk). Thetford (Nf), Tetford (L).

þing, OE, ON, 'meeting, assembly, court.' Thinghill (He), Tingley (Y), from *Thinglaw*, Finedon (Nth), Fingest (Bk). It is significant that in each case it is compounded with a word denoting a hill.

þing-vǫllr, ON, 'place of assembly,' a p.n. used in Iceland of the place of meeting of the Allthing or parliament. Thingwall (La, Ch).

þorn, OE, ON, '*thorn*-bush.' Places whose name begins with *Thorn*- must for the most part have been so called owing to the presence of some thorn-bush close at hand, but some *Thorntons* and the like may denote enclosures actually made from thorn-bushes. Bythorne (Hu), Shuckton (Db).

þorp, OE, or, much more commonly, þrop, ON þorp, ODan. thorp, in one form and another, are fairly common in England but their distribution is unequal. The suffix is fairly common in Gl, O, W, Ha, Berks, Bk and found occasionally in Do, So, St, Wo, Wa, Sr, while it is apparently unknown in D, Wt, K, Mx, He, Sa, Ch. Then it is very common in Y (much more so in the East than in the North and West Ridings), L, Lei, Nt, Nth, R, Nf and slightly less common in Db, Hu, Sf, We, while it is occasionally found in Ess, Beds, Herts, .Du, La and is unknown in Nb, Cu, C. This grouping suggests (i) that there were two centres of distribution of the suffix, so to speak, one in the South Midlands, the other in Scand. England, and (ii) that, with the exception of a few examples in We, the suffix in Scand. England must be of Danish rather than Norse origin. The twofold origin of this suffix is confirmed by its form. In the first group of counties it is very rarely found in the form *thorp* at all. We find such forms as Thrupp (Berks), Throope (W), Souldrop (Beds), Astrop (O), Williamstrip, Hatherop, Pin-drup (Gl), Huntingtrap (Wo), all going back to ME *thrope* and OE þrop(þ). In the other group it is very rare to get anything except a *thorp*-form and this must go back to the Scand. form.

þorp, OE, is found in very early glosses as an alternative to **tun** and as the equivalent of Lat. *competum*, 'cross-roads,' *fundus*, 'estate,' *villa*, 'farm,' and also as an alternative to *þingstow*, 'place of assembly.' It is as difficult to be precise about its meaning as about that of *tun*. It is perhaps best rendered 'village' or 'hamlet,' though medieval usage suggests that in names of late origin it was generally used of some smaller form of settlement.

þorp, ON, denotes a group of homesteads, perhaps also a farm or croft, but as the word in England seems to be of Danish origin rather than Norse we should perhaps look rather to the meaning of ODan. *thorp*, 'smaller village due to colonisation from a larger one.' That is certainly its significance in the numerous cases like Welwick Thorpe (Y) in which we have *Thorpe* added to a village name.

þræll, ON, '*thrall*, serf.' Threlkeld (Cu), Trailholme (La).

þveit, ON, lit. 'piece cut out or off,' hence 'parcel of land, clearing, paddock.' In NCy it is still used, and describes 'a forest clearing, a low meadow, the shelving part of a mountain side, a single house or hamlet.' In p.n. it is very common in Cu, We, North La, West Y, and a great deal less common in the rest of Scand. England. See Ekwall, *PN La* 19, and also a full discussion in Lindkvist, *PN Scand. Origin* 96 ff. Lindkvist shows that most of the names containing this element are probably of comparatively recent origin, representing new land taken into cultivation, at first often only a field. Its commonness in the North-West and its comparative rarity elsewhere may perhaps be due not so much to difference of race, as between Norse and Danes, as to the fact that the Midland districts were already more fully cultivated when the Viking settlers came. It is usually written in the full form *thwaite* in the suffixes of p.n. in the North-West, but pronounced [θət]. In districts where it is less common it is subject to alteration and corruption as in Swathwick (Db), Crostwick, Guestwick (Nf), Eastwood (Nt), Brackenfield (Db), Stainfield in Kesteven (L), Braworth (Y).

*þwīt, OE, or *þvīt, ON, is postulated by Ekwall to explain names like Inglewhite (La), Trewhitt (Nb), Crostwight (Nf). It would be allied to þveit and have something of the same sense.

þȳrel, OE, 'pierced, hollow.' Thurlestone (D), Thirlwall (Nb).

þyrne, OE, 'thorn-bush.' Thurne (Nf), Thearne (Y). Dat. pl. in Thurnham (La), Farnham (Nb). Caistron (Nb), Casterne (St), Chawston (Beds), Winster (Db), Baythorne End (Ess). In Scand. England it is impossible to distinguish it from ON þyrnir.

þyrs, OE, þurs, ON, 'giant.' Thirsden, Thursclough, Thrushgill (La).

ticcen, OE, 'kid.' Titchwell (Nf), Ticehurst (Sx), Tisted (Ha).

tigel, OE, '*tile*.' Tyley Bottom (Gl), Tilehurst (Berks).

timber, OE, ON, '*timber*.' Timberland (L), Nyetimber (Sx), Timberdine (Wo).

tiǫrn, ON, '*tarn*.'

topt, ON, 'piece of ground, messuage, homestead.' Such are also the senses of its descendant *toft*. Cf. 'with toft and croft,' in which *toft* refers to the homestead, **croft** to the land attached. The term came also to be used of a field or piece of land generally, not necessarily the site of a house. The root-idea of the word is that of a 'clearing,' more especially on high or exposed ground. Cf. dial. *toft*, used of a knoll or hillock. See more fully *PN Scand. Origin* 208 ff. As the word was in common use in ME it is not a definite test of Scand. settlement. It is Danish rather than Norwegian and is commonest in L, Nf, Y.

torr, OE, 'high rock, pile of rocks, rocky peak, hill, dial. *tor* (D, Co, Db).' Ekwall (ES 54, 108–110) shows it to be a Celtic loanword. Dunster (So), Notter (Co), Hay Tor (D).

trani, ON, 'crane.' Tranmere (Ch), Trenholme (Y), Tarnacre

(La). See more fully Ekwall in NoB 8, 94. In some cases it may be a nickname.

trēo(w), OE, '*tree.*' Oswestry (Sa), Austrey (Wa), Holmstrow (Sx), Cator, Trewe (D). It is not always easy to distinguish it from trog.

trog, OE, '*trough*, conduit,' but used also in a topographical sense as in the '*Trough* of Bowland' (Y). Not always easy to distinguish from **treo**. Trafford (Ch), Trawden (La), Trowes (Nb).

trynde, OE, 'round lump,' allied to which there must have been an adj. form which in p.n. could describe something which is 'circular' as in Trindhurst (K), Tryndehayes (Ess), Trindle Down (Berks), Trundle Mere (C), Trundlebeer, Trendwell (D). Some of these p.n. may contain OE *trindæl*, which Grundy takes to be a compound of *trinde* and **dæl**.

tūn, OE, is the commonest of all p.n. suffixes and it is clear from its OE usage generally that it must have a wide range of meaning in p.n. Its primary sense is 'enclosed piece of ground' and that is its meaning in such compounds as **æppeltun, leactun, gærstun**. From that it came to mean 'enclosed land with dwellings on it, estate, manor, vill, village.' These are probably its meanings in the vast majority of p.n. The idea of some lord's authority over the *tun* is implied in such phrases as *mannes tun, eorles tun* and *cyninges tun* (= villa regia), whence numerous *Kingstons*, and the fact that in 859 you could make a grant of a *healf tun* (BCS 497) suggests that by this time the enclosure-idea may have been weakened. As early as the 7th century, in the Laws of the Kentish Hlothere and Eadric we find *tun* implying a community of persons, for the thief is to be cleared by the oaths of persons from the *tun* to which he belongs. Similarly in the Laws of Aethelstan a certain fine is to be divided among the poor who are in the *tun*. In another passage in the Laws (ed. Liebermann, p. 453) we hear how the reeve should have cognisance of what happens both in *tun* and *dun*, in which the contrast seems to be between the dwellings of men as found in the *tun* and the open uninhabited country on the *dun* or hill. So similarly *toune* is used in ME of the dwellings of men generally. As noted under **ham** there is at least one passage in OE in which it seems to be definitely contrasted with that word and to be used of a smaller unit, at least so far as population is concerned. There is no reason for thinking that in p.n. it was ever in early times used with the sense 'town,' which it undoubtedly has in some OE passages, more especially in translations from Latin. Its most common Latin equivalent is *villa* and the best general rendering would seem to be 'farm' or even 'manor.' Traces of the older senses of *tun* are still to be found in dial. *town*, 'farmstead and its buildings' (Sc.) and 'cluster of houses,' especially those round the church, very common in various parts of the country and in America.

tūnsteall, OE, = **tun** + **steall,** would seem to have been used in much the same sense as *hamsteall,* viz. farm and its buildings, farmstead. Tunstal(l) *passim,* Dunstall (L), Tounstal (D).

tūnstede, OE, = **tun** + **stede,** is used in the same sense as **tunsteall.** Tunste(a)d *passim.*

twī-, OE, 'double.' Twyford *passim,* from OE *twi-fyrde,* lit. 'with a double ford,' found also in Twerton (So), Tiverton (D). Twywell (Nth).

twisla, OE, 'fork.' Used in p.n. of the fork where two streams meet. Twizel (Nb), Twiston, Bastwell (La), Haltwhistle (Nb), Briestwistle (Y).

ufera, OE, 'upper.' West Overton (W), Overpool (Ch).

ūle, OE, '*owl.*' Ulcombe (K), Oldcoats (Nt), Outchester (Nb).

úlfr, ON, 'wolf.' Ulpha (Cu, We). Difficult to distinguish from the pers. name *Ulfr.*

upp(e), OE, '*up,* above.' Upavon (W), Tipton (Co). (See under æt.)

vangr, ON, '*campus.*' The Swed. cognate is used of a cultivated field. Wetwang (Y).

varða, varði, ON, 'cairn, heap of stones.' Warcopp (We), Warbreck (La).

vað, ON, 'ford,' cognate with **wæd.** Langwith (Db, Nt, Y), Langworth, Waithe (L), Solway, Langwathby (Cu).

veggr, ON, 'wall.' Stanwix (Cu) and possibly in Stanwick (Nth, Y).

veiðr, ON, 'fishing, hunting, place for such.' Wedholme (Cu), Waitham (La).

vík, ON, 'bay, creek,' NCy *wick,* used of a creek or inlet and often applied in the form *wyke* to the small bays on Lakes Windermere, Esthwaite and Coniston[1]. One may get it inland on the shores of a mere or on land which was once a mere, as in Blowick (La)[1]. Careful topographical study is needed in Scand. England to distinguish it from *wick* from **wic.** It may possibly also be used of a 'nook or corner in the hills.' Rygh (*Indledning* s.v.) notes the possibility of such in Norway and this would agree with the further NCy use of *wick* to denote a 'corner, angle, hollow.'

viðr, ON, 'wood.' Skirwith (Y). A good many names in *with* really go back to **vað.**

(v)rá, ON, 'nook, corner,' dial. *wray* (We), used of a remote or secluded spot. Wreay, Sillyrea, Stanger (Cu), Haverah (H), Bramery (Cu), Wray (La), Dockray (Cu), Scarrow (Cu).

---

[1] From information kindly given by Mr F. H. Cheetham, F.S.A.

wād, OE, '*woad*.' Wadborough (Wo), Woodhill, Whaddon (W), Odell (Beds).

wæd, OE, 'ford,' cognate with **vað**. Landwade (C), Wadebridge (Co).

(ge)wæsc, OE, 'ground washed over by water, ford,' and, in the compound *sceap-wæsc*, 'place for washing sheep.' Sheepwash (Nb), Shipston-on-Stour (Wo), Strangeways (La). Formerly thought to be found also in Alrewas, Hopwas (St), Rotherwas (He) and other similar names, but Ritter (*op. cit.* 71–2) raises certain difficulties which have not yet been solved and there is the further possibility in the unstressed suffix that we may have to do with OE *wāse*, 'mud, *ooze*.'

wǣt, OE, '*wet*.' Weetwood (Nb), Wheatshaw (La).

ware, OE, 'inhabitants,' not used independently. Canterbury (K), Clewer (Berks, So), Burmarsh (K).

wēala, OE, gen. pl. of *wealh*, 'foreigner, Welshman, serf,' often applied by the English to the Britons. Very common in numerous Waltons, Walworths, Walcotes. Wherever we find them we probably have traces either of a distinctive survival of the old Celtic population for a short time at least after the English Conquest or of settlements of British servants belonging to some large estate. Wawcott (Berks).

weald, wald, OE, is certainly used in OE of forest-land and more especially of high forest-land. In ME it developes forms *we(e)ld* and *wold* in different dialects and the meaning is by no means so clear. *we(e)ld* seems for the most part to have kept its old sense but *wold* came frequently to be used of waste ground, wide open country, still, as in the *Cotswolds* and the Yorkshire and Lincolnshire *Wolds*, on high ground. The change from wooded to open country has its parallel in the development of **leah**, the term having been transferred from the forest to the ground which has been cleared of forest. In names of comparatively recent origin we should hardly be right in assuming that the ground must necessarily ever have been wooded at all. Hammill, Ringwould (K), Wield (Ha), Weald (Ess), Old, Walgrave (Nth), Oldridge (D), Old Hurst, Old Weston (Hu), Horninghold (Lei). For the dial. development v. Ekwall, *Contrib. to Hist. of OE Dial.* 5 ff.

weall, OE, '*wall*.' Wall (Nb, St).

weard, OE, 'watch, *ward*.' Wardlow (Db), Wardle (Ch).

weg, OE, '*way*, path, road.' Holloway (Mx), Wickey (Beds).

welig, wylig, OE, '*willow*.' Willey Hund., Willington (Beds), Willitoft (Y). Dat. pl. in Welwyn (Herts), Willen (Bk).

(ge)weorc, OE, 'fort, defensive work.' Aldwark (Y), Newark (Nt, Sr), Foremark (Db).

wer, OE, '*weir*.' Weare (So), Edgware (Mx), Wear Gifford (D), Wareham (Do).

west, OE, *'west.'* Comparative form in Westerfield (Sf), superl. in Westmeston (Sx).

whin, ME, 'gorse, *whin.'* Probably a Scand. loan-word. See Ekwall, *PN La* 20. Whinfell (Cu), Whinburgh (Nf).

wīc, OE, denotes primarily 'dwelling-place, abode, quarters,' and is very commonly used in the plural. It is clear from such glosses as *wic* vel *lytel port* (v. **port**), *castellum, vicus* that it also developed the meaning 'village.' From its use in the compound *wic-gerefa*, the name of some kind of king's officer in Saxon times, it is evident also that the word must have acquired a more or less definite technical sense. In Domesday, especially in Essex, it often has the meaning 'dairy-farm,' a sense in which it survived locally until the 16th cent. In p.n. in OE we find it in the compounds **berewic** and **heordwic** where the 'farm' sense of *wic* must be prominent as also in *gatawic* (from **gat**), *oxenawic* and *sceapwic*, from which we have the p.n. Gatwick (Sr), Oxwick (Nf), Shapwick (So).

In BCS 129 we have mention of a grant *in Wico emptorio quem nos Saltwich vocamus* (14th cent. copy) and this passage has been used to support the view that OE *wic* might also denote a brine-spring, but the passage does not necessarily imply that. It is a well-known fact that in the Worcestershire Droitwich and in the Cheshire Nantwich, Northwich, and Middlewich we have p.n. in *-wich* for places in which, at least in the present day, there are salt-workings, while in dial. glossaries the term *wich* is sometimes equated with 'salt-works.' The association with salt is however purely a chance one and the *wic* only refers to the buildings which sprang up around the salt-workings[1].

Grundy has noted that this element is comparatively rarely compounded with a pers. name and this fact points to its denoting as a rule something which belongs to a community rather than to an individual. The *wick* was often the dairy farm of the community.

It is a loan-word from the Lat. *vicus* and its normal phonological development should be to Mod. Eng. *wich*, from OE *wic*, which was pronounced with a palatal *c*. Forms in *wick* are however much more common in Mod. Eng. than those in *wich*. Apart from the general confusion of palatalised and non-palatalised forms of such words in present-day speech, there is a special reason for confusion in p.n. in *wic*. The word was much more common in the pl. than in the sg. in OE, and such forms as *wican, wicum* (dat. pl.) would keep the *c* unpalatalised, whence it would be extended

---

[1] The statements given above have since been more than confirmed by very full and precise evidence as to *wick* and *wich* in Wo, kindly placed at my disposal by Mr F. T. S. Houghton, F.S.A.

to other forms of the same word. It would be unsafe therefore to draw any conclusions as to palatalisation of OE *c* from the distribution of *wich* and *wick* forms. The normal development is to *wich* or *wick* but sometimes, especially when the word is used independently as a p.n. we have the form *wyke* and, in the South-West, *week*. Forms like Wyken (Wa), Wicken (C) are from the dat. pl. In Scand. England it is often difficult to distinguish it from **vik**. Quickbury (Ess).

The suggestion has sometimes been made that there was another OE *wic*, denoting 'bay, creek,' the English counterpart of **vik** and that this lies behind such p.n. as Sandwich, Greenwich, Woolwich (K), Harwich (Ess), but apart from names of places like this, which are on estuaries or creeks or bays, there is no evidence for the existence of such a word in OE and as these names are all capable of explanation with the ordinary *wic*, we should probably rest content with that. Guttridge (Ess), Cowage (W), Wix (Ess), Swanage (Do).

wice, OE, '*wych*-elm,' is very difficult to distinguish from **wic**.

wīcham and **wīchamm**, OE, for both forms are found in OE, are the source of several *Wickhams*. Their exact significance is obscure. Do they denote 'farms' or 'enclosures' by a *wic*, and is it possible, in some cases at least, that the *wic* is really a Roman *vicus*, for there are a good many cases in which Wickhams are by Roman remains?

wīcing, OE, 'pirate, viking,' probably, as suggested by Craigie, one who takes up his *wic* or quarters in some other land. The word was in use in England long before the actual coming of the Vikings, though that term is its Norse equivalent. The OE word or the ON *viking* or the same word used as a pers. name is found in Wigston Magna (Lei), Wickenby (L), Whissonsett (Nf).

wīd, OE, '*wide*,' is often very difficult to distinguish from **wiðig**.

wielle, wiella, OE, **wælle, wælla**, Angl., 'spring, *well*.' These should develop respectively in later English to *well* and *wall* but the *wall* forms have survived but rarely, as in Craswall (He). Usually they have been replaced by St. Eng. forms, as in Bradwell (St). Nom. pl. in Wells (Nf, So), dat. pl. in Welham (Nt). See more fully Ekwall, *Contrib. Hist. OE Dial.* 4 ff. Colwall (He), Satchfield, Halwill (D), Dewsall, Cobhall (He), Astol (Sa), Sneachill (Wo), Hassal, Thelwall (Ch), Rusthall (K), Bexfield (Ess).

wilde, OE, '*wild*.' Eyton-on-the-Weald-Moors (Sa), Willand (D).

wincel, OE, 'nook, corner, angle,' only found in p.n. Winchcomb (Gl, K), Aldwinkle (Nth).

winter, OE, '*winter*,' used in Wintercote (Ha) of that which is 'used in winter' and in the numerous Winterbournes in South-

West England of a stream which is only worthy of the name in that season.

wisc, OE, 'damp meadow, marsh, *wish* (dial.).' Only found in charter material. Cranwich (Nf), Dulwich (Sr), Wissington (Sf), Whistley (Berks), Sledwick (Du).

wiðig, OE, '*withy.*' Hoarwithy (He), Weethley (Wa), Weeton (La, Y), Widford (Gl), Widdecombe (D), Woodbatch (Sa), Wissington (Sf). Often difficult to distinguish from **wid.**

wōh, OE, 'crooked, twisting.' Woburn (Beds), Wooburn (Bk), Oborne (Do). Wonersh (Sr) shows the weak dat. sg. *wo(h)an.*

worþ, weorþ, wyrþ, OE, is only found in p.n. material in OE and in a few Biblical glosses. In the former we have grants of land at various places bearing names with this suffix and the estate is variously rendered in the Latin as *villula, villa, viculus, aliquantulum terrae, aliquam telluris partem.* In the latter it is used to render the Lat. *atrium* and *platea.* From the frequent mention of a **hege** in connexion with a *worþ,* it would seem that the latter, like its derivative **worðig** denoted an enclosed area and this is confirmed by the similar use of the LGerm. *word, wurd.* The Latin renderings, in contrast to those of **tun** and **ham** suggest that it was used of a relatively small enclosure. The fact that it is not found in independent use in OE tends to show that it was obsolescent soon after the Saxon Conquest and there is no evidence that it was in living use at the time of the Norman Conquest. It is fairly evenly distributed throughout the country, except that it is not found in Cu, We, and is very rare in the North and East Riding of Y. In D it often gives place to the allied **worðig** and in the West Midlands to **worðign.** In the unstressed suffix position it is often liable to corruption as in Clarewood (Nb), Pertwood (W), Duxford (C), Barkwith (L), Ember (Sr). See further Ekwall *PN La* 20–1.

worðig, OE, an expanded form of **worþ,** with which it often interchanges in p.n. There is an excellent discussion of it in BT s.v. It is clear from the statements in the Laws about the necessity for a ceorl's putting a *tun* or hedge round his *worðig* that the primary idea is that of an enclosure. It is used as a gloss for Lat. *agellus, fundus, praedium.* The chief home of this suffix is D and So and it must have continued in living use a good deal later than **worþ,** to judge by the large number of p.n. in the Exeter Domesday in which this element is compounded with the name of the actual holder of the estate TRE or TRW. It is found in King's and Martyr Worthy (Ha), has been replaced by *worth* in Tamworth (St) and was once found in *Norþworþig* Db, the old name of Derby itself. A good many of the *worthys* in D, on the other hand, were originally *worths.*

worðign, OE, an expanded form of **worðig** and used with the same meaning. It survives in dial. *worthine* (He), 'a division of land.' See further Schlutter in Anglia, 43, 99–100. It usually appears as *wardine* in p.n. but is found in other forms in Marden (He), Ruardean (Gl), Northenden (Ch), Ellerdine (Sa). In a good many names it was once found but has now been replaced by the more common *worth* or some development of it, as in Minster-worth (Gl), Chickward, Strongwood (He). The suffix is confined to Ch, Sa, He, Gl, Wa except for a few cases in D, where some of the p.n. which now end in *worthy* once had this suffix, e.g. Badgeworthy, Bradworthy. It is just possible that it is found in Worthing (Nf).

wrang, Late OE, 'twisted, crooked,' a Scand. loan-word. Wrangdyke Hund. (R).

wrīd, wrīþ, OE, 'thicket, *ride* (dial.),' only in charter material. Easwrith Hund. (Sx), Wordwell (Sf).

wudu, OE, 'wood.' Very common in *wudu-tun*, later *Wo(o)tton* and *Woodhouse*. Manhood (Sx), Wothersome (Y).

wulf, OE, '*wolf*,' is very difficult to distinguish from pers. names formed with the same element, but we certainly have the gen. pl. *wulfa* in Woolpit (Sf) and a good many *Woolleys*.

wyrt, OE, 'vegetable, *wort*.' Worton (Mx, O).

yfre, OE, is only found in charter material in OE. Etymologically it would seem to be identical with Goth. *ubizwa*, itself closely related to OE *efes*, 'eaves.' If this is correct its meaning may well be that of 'edge' or (as Grundy on other grounds suggests) 'escarpment.' It survives in two or three p.n. in the form River (Sx) and Rivar (W). v. æt.

CAMBRIDGE: PRINTED BY W. LEWIS AT THE UNIVERSITY PRESS

ENGLISH PLACE-NAME SOCIETY

founded to carry out the

SURVEY OF ENGLISH PLACE-NAMES

UNDERTAKEN WITH THE APPROVAL AND
ENCOURAGEMENT OF THE BRITISH ACADEMY

PRESIDENT

PROFESSOR JAMES TAIT, M.A., LITT.D., F.B.A.

VICE-PRESIDENTS

PROFESSOR W. A. CRAIGIE, M.A., LL.D.
J. H. ROUND, M.A., LL.D.
W. H. STEVENSON, M.A.

COUNCIL

O. G. S. CRAWFORD, B.A., F.S.A.
PROFESSOR E. EKWALL, PH.D.
REV. CANON C. W. FOSTER, M.A., F.S.A.
PROFESSOR J. FRASER, M.A.
WM. PAGE, F.S.A.
MISS A. C. PAUES, PH.D.
PROFESSOR W. J. SEDGEFIELD, M.A., LITT.D.
PROFESSOR F. M. STENTON, M.A.

HON. SECRETARY AND DIRECTOR OF THE SURVEY

PROFESSOR A. MAWER, M.A.

HON. TREASURER

COL. SIR CHARLES CLOSE, K.B.E., F.R.S.

HON. GENERAL EDITORS

PROFESSOR MAWER   PROFESSOR STENTON

THE MINIMUM ANNUAL SUBSCRIPTION TO THE SOCIETY
IS 15s. AND ENTITLES MEMBERS TO RECEIVE
THE SOCIETY'S ANNUAL VOLUME

ALL ENQUIRIES & COMMUNICATIONS SHOULD BE ADDRESSED TO

The Hon. Sec., English Place-name Society
The University, Liverpool